OUTLAWS and LAWMEN of the WEST

Volume II

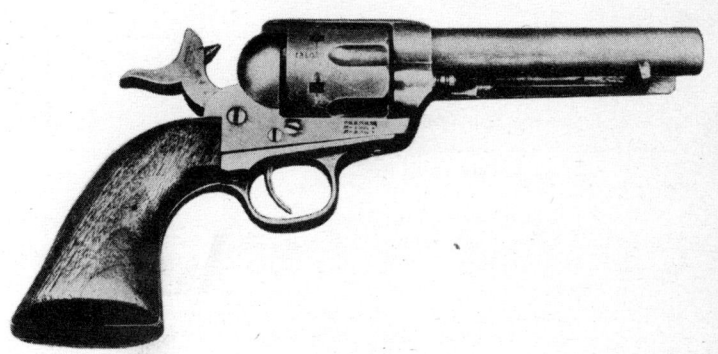

Dan Asfar

LONE PINE

© 2001 by Lone Pine Publishing
First printed in 2001   10 9 8 7 6 5 4 3 2 1
Printed in Canada

All rights reserved. No part of this work covered by the copyrights hereon may be reproduced or used in any form or by any means–graphic, electronic or mechanical–without the prior written permission of the publisher, except for reviewers, who may quote brief passages. Any request for photocopying, recording, taping or storage on information retrieval systems of any part of this work shall be directed in writing to the publisher.

The Publisher: Lone Pine Publishing

1901 Raymond Ave. SW, Suite C   10145 - 81 Avenue
Renton, WA 98055   Edmonton, AB T6E 1W9
USA   Canada

Website: www.lonepinepublishing.com

National Library of Canada Cataloguing in Pubication Data

Macpherson, M.A. (Margaret A.), 1959—
    Outlaws and lawmen of the West

    Volume 2 written by Dan Asfar.
    ISBN 1-55105-164-8 (v. 1)—ISBN 1-551-5-338-1 (v. 2)

    1. Outlaws–West (U.S.)–History—19th century. I. MacLaren, E. (Eli) II. Asfar, Dan, 1973—III. Title.
HV6785.M32 2000   364.1'092'278   C200-910241-8

Editorial Director: Nancy Foulds
Editorial: Randy Williams, Dawn Loewen, Eli MacLaren
Illustrations Coordinator: Carol Woo
Production Manager: Jody Reekie
Layout & Production: Monica Triska
Book Design: Heather Markham
Cover Design: Robert Weidemann
Cover Illustration: Image Club Graphics
Maps: Arlana Anderson-Hale

Photographs used in this book are reproduced with the generous permission of the following copyright holders: Arizona Historical Society (p. 16, #61664; pp. 36–37, #42005; p. 40, #27218); Denver Public Library, Western History/Genealogy Department (p. 132); Kansas State Historical Society (pp. 24–25, 28, 64, 82, 110, 128–129, 158); Glenn Shirley (p. 212); University of Oklahoma Library/Western History Collections, Rose Collection (Title page, #2278; p. 48, #2740; p. 155, #2152; p. 209, #1776; p. 239, #2040).

Photographs on pages 186 and 191 are from *A Cowboy Detective*, by Charles Siringo (W.B. Conkey Company, 1912; reprinted by University of Nebraska Press, 1988).

We acknowledge the financial support of the Government of Canada through the Book Publishing Industry Development Program (BPIDP) for our publishing activities.

PC: P6

CONTENTS

Acknowledgments 4
Dedication 4
Foreword 5

1 Wyatt Earp 16

2 Bill Longley 47

3 Dave Mather 64

4 Bat Masterson 81

5 Luke Short 110

6 Ben Thompson 132

7 Wild Bill Hickok 157

8 Charlie Siringo 185

9 Bill Doolin 211

ACKNOWLEDGMENTS

While storytellers may do fine by themselves when telling their tales around the dinner tables, campfires and water coolers of the world, books are never the products of one person's work alone.

I would like to thank the people at Lone Pine Publishing for their invaluable support and assistance in the completion of this book–particularly Shane Kennedy and Nancy Foulds, for their enthusiasm and interest in the six-gun scoundrels who blighted American history; Carol Woo, for unearthing pictures of many of these legendary figures in their Sunday best; and Randy Williams and Dawn Loewen, for shaking the burrs out of these stories and teaching me a thing or two about how words go together to boot. Thanks.

DEDICATION

For Teta, Mom and Rita.

FOREWORD

As to killing, I never think much about it. I don't believe in ghosts, and I don't keep the lights burning all night to keep them away. That's because I'm not a murderer. It is the other man or me in a fight and I never stop to think, "Is it a sin to do this thing?" And after it is done, what's the use of disturbing the mind?

–Wild Bill Hickok

Whether Wild Bill Hickok was a cold-blooded murderer or a man forced into lethal action by his sense of duty and instinct for self-preservation depends on whose book you are reading. Pistol-twirling madman or a 19th-century knight without armor? The question itself overlooks the larger reality of the man and his times.

Wild Bill was delighted with the reputation lent by his numerous killings. Whatever attitude he may have had while thinning the population of western towns, the gunfighter was for the most part proud of his grisly accomplishments–and his contemporaries stoked this pride with heaping measures of fear, respect and adoration. Though Wild Bill had a mean streak a mile wide, it has been said that the cause of human behavior lies somewhere between nature and nurture. And whatever one may think about the man himself, the austere and often merciless country he inhabited did little to temper his personal demons.

Hickok's world was a hard place, one that could grind the virtue out of a pious man, turn a smiling soul sour and prod a kindhearted disposition into bitter intemperance. It was in the Wild West that the ideals of a "civilized" eastern society collided with an alien and largely unwelcoming frontier. The American concepts of "manifest destiny" and "pursuit of happiness" transformed an entire population into frantic fortune seekers whose boundless ambitions were checked only by the finite resources the land contained—and by the threat of violence from others who were after the same spoils. Engaging in gold rushes, silver rushes, land rushes and cattle drives, the man of the West was an opportunist, moiling to dig, drive or harvest a profit from the landscape. And God have mercy on anything that got in his way.

It was clear from the onset that Americans were deadly serious about expansion. To feed settlers' voracious hunger for land, President Andrew Jackson's administration oversaw the expulsion of the Choctaws, Chickasaws, Creeks, Seminoles and Cherokees from their traditional lands east of the Mississippi. By the mid-1830s, all of the Five Civilized Tribes had been relocated in the newly formed and federally run Indian Territory in what is now Oklahoma. Meanwhile, American settlers in nearby Texas were growing so confident in their increased numbers that they would rebel against the Mexican authorities in 1835, winning independence as a republic in a short, bloody rebellion. When the United States annexed Texas in 1846, another war with Mexico broke out. Americans were again victorious, and the U.S. wrested control of all Mexican territory north of the Rio Grande, including California and New Mexico, with the Treaty of Guadalupe Hidalgo in 1848. The treaty dramatically expanded American holdings in the West, adding present-day Utah, Nevada, Arizona and much of Colorado and Wyoming to the land within its borders.

Fortune hunters came close behind the military. Gold was discovered near Sacramento, California, in 1848, and it was not long before a disease called "gold fever" infected thousands of men around the world. There was a veritable stampede for California; the non-Native population of the state shot up from 14,000 in 1848 to 223,856 in 1852. This first wave of migrants made up a rough society of mostly rootless young men whose first love was glittering metal. It was a love that often went unrequited, and thousands of the hopefuls who swarmed to the hills became bitter, drunken regulars at the saloons that proliferated in the murderous mining camps. Grudges and gambling debts accumulated with innumerable jealousies, and crime rates soared as men got lost in the dark subculture of the sporting world.

The successive gold and silver rushes in Colorado, Nevada, Idaho and Montana never created the same level of pandemonium as that caused by the California Forty-niners, but the difference was only a matter of degree. The restless hordes of prospectors who swarmed to each new discovery of precious metal consistently created an atmosphere of lawlessness and violence.

Most Indians cared very little about white America's obsession with gold–until 1874, that is, when a rich vein was discovered around the Black Hills in South Dakota. The hills were sacred ground for the Lakota Sioux and were lawfully theirs according to the 1868 Treaty of Fort Laramie. So when miners began flooding into the region under army protection, the martial tribes of the Sioux Confederacy went to war against the United States–not for rights to the mineral wealth in the Black Hills, but to protect their land, and the way of life that went with it, from an encroaching foreign population. It was to be the last round of warfare for mastery of the Great Plains, ending in the final defeat of the Plains Indians, and the complete eradication of the nomadic culture they lived by.

According to white Americans, Native populations figured prominently in what was wild about the West. From the first days of American settlement on the Atlantic seaboard, taming the land also meant subjugating the indigenous peoples who inhabited it; depending on the time and place, the "uncivilized Indian" could be either an obstacle or an aid to wealth-seeking European immigrants. But as white settlers began to move past the 100th meridian in the latter half of the 19th century, they found themselves pushing up against the expanding and extremely militant horse and gun culture of the Plains Indian. The nomadic Sioux posed the greatest threat to the westward expansion of the United States. Attacking settlements, outposts, soldiers and pioneers up and down the frontier, the highly skilled warriors of the Sioux Confederacy had every man, woman and child from Texas to the Dakota Territory fearing for their scalps. It was during the government's campaigns against the fierce Plains Indians that many of the West's six-gun elite received their training as killers–employed as scouts and buffalo hunters in the bloody struggles on the prairie.

But Indians were not the only catalysts for violence in the region. Along with their spades, hoes, shovels and wagons, eastern settlers brought considerable political baggage to the frontier, and the divisive politics of the settled East quickly exploded into open conflict in the unsettled West. The issue of slavery had split the United States into two distinct cultures: the free-labor states of the North and the slave-centered economy of the South. If the two societies had reached some sort of tenuous balance during the first half of the 19th century, the question of the western territories' future created an environment of barely restrained hostility in Washington, D.C. Would the territories be made into free or slave states? Though Congress attempted a number of legislative bills to peaceably divide the territories, the matter turned bloody when the general population got involved in the issue. When the citizens of

Kansas were called upon to decide the future of their new state in 1854, the region erupted in violence. Kansas and neighboring Missouri boiled under the heat of the conflict until the onset of the Civil War in 1861.

If four years of brutal warfare killed the political will to fight, it also did very little to quell regional differences. The war ended in 1865; the Reconstruction years that followed were marred by countless grievances. The Southern states, humiliated and economically devastated, produced an entire class of bitter Civil War veterans, unemployed but well armed, who had grown numb to violence. Many of these men drifted to the West, where the law was fragile, almost everyone was armed and most of the socializing took place in saloons. North continued to meet South in the dissolute setting of western watering holes, and the lasting ire of the Civil War was played out in more than one gunfight on the frontier.

The most famous example of these tensions was to be found in the burgeoning cattle trade. When Confederate soldiers returned to Texas from eastern battlefields, they found that wild longhorn cattle had proliferated in their absence. An estimated five million head of beef were roaming southern Texas by the end of the war. So, with a vigor driven by the economic desperation of the post-war South, Texan entrepreneurs began rounding the longhorns into massive herds, inaugurating the expansive cattle business that dominated the western economy for over two decades.

These cattle were driven to the stockyards in Kansas towns every spring. The early cattle drives stamped municipalities such as Abilene, Ellsworth and Dodge City into the books of American legend. With the sudden influx of rowdy Texans swarming the small western towns came unparalleled bouts of roaring revelry that lasted all summer. But with Southern men pouring into a state that had fought for the Union not too many years back, it was often difficult to tell if the Texans were carousing or warring when they arrived at trail's end.

The golden age of the cattle industry would quickly pass into history as the short grass that had sustained the Texas longhorns was used up, the railroads expanded farther west and the land became fenced by increasing numbers of farmers. While the homesteader was definitely a much tamer resident than the cowpuncher, even the relatively disciplined farmers of the West were responsible for their fair share of bedlam.

By 1889, the Indian Territory set aside for Natives by Andrew Jackson's administration in 1830 was one of the last remaining tracts of unsettled land left in the West. When the territory was opened for white settlement at precisely 12 PM on April 22, 1889, the ensuing rush for land turned downright ugly. Chaos ensued at the stroke of noon as thousands of would-be homesteaders stampeded across the border to claim their 160 acres. During the last decade of the 19th century, the Indian Territory gradually became known as the Oklahoma Territory and six-gun outlawry in the region rose to dramatic levels. The criminals who infested this region in the 1890s would be counted among the last outlaws of the Old West.

Outlaws and lawmen both, the men who settled the West were individuals who—whether through strength of character, natural inclination or sheer perversion—thrived on the hard conditions of frontier America. These were men who were confident, detached or crazy enough to greet harrowing situations with an impressive degree of calm. The inner forces that drove these men during their exploits propelled their often-murderous careers into the annals of American legend. Outlaw and lawman alike would become popular icons from an era that was defined by violence.

Wyatt Earp was an individual who had a deep faith in this place. He believed that if a man was hard enough, he could make himself a fortune in the harsh landscape west of the Missouri. But even though his own hunt for riches took him all over the West, put him to work in a great number of different occupations and landed him in the middle of the legendary gunfight at the OK Corral, Wyatt Earp never did find his fortune. Earp outlasted the Wild West and lived to old age, but he was always reluctant to sell the one valuable thing he owned, the thing that would eventually make other men millions of dollars: his life's story.

Bill Longley was just no good. He pretty much lived life on the lam after committing his first murder at the age of 15, and his next 11 years consisted of one long killing spree. Whatever merciless form of madness twisted his mind, it was able to flourish in the ugly conditions in Texas after the Civil War. Virulently racist and violently anti-social, this roving mankiller's gun almost always came to life when he was in the company of others. It has been estimated that by the time Longley was captured in 1877, at least 32 men had been felled by his six-shooters.

It is difficult to say if Mysterious Dave Mather was a simpleton or a man of profound depth, but one thing is certain: The laconic gunfighter knew how to shoot. Wandering the West without pause or purpose, Mather was just as comfortable wearing the silver star as he was running from it. Dave's only apparent goal in life was to accumulate as many sins as he could, perhaps in an attempt to defy the memory of his Holy-Rolling progenitor, famed New England theologian Cotton Mather.

Bat Masterson's résumé in the rough world west of the Missouri was impressive. Whether he was working as a laborer, buffalo hunter, scout, gambler, lawman, fight promoter or journalist, he was consistently a leader among men. Masterson made headlines wherever he went–from his tenure as sheriff of Dodge County to his stint as a boxing promoter in Denver to his days as a sports columnist and personal confidant to former president Theodore Roosevelt in New York City. The sheer breadth of this legendary gunfighter's experience made him one of North America's most celebrated characters.

Luke Short was a man who thrived in the amoral sporting world of the West because he always kept his eye on the bottom line. Money, not excitement, was Luke's first love—and no law, moral code or pistol-packing badman could distract him from the smell of greenbacks.

Degenerate Texan Ben Thompson was afflicted with a rover's disposition and had a fierce love for whiskey, cards and violence. But unlike so many others who were swallowed up by the vices of the sporting world, Thompson enjoyed an impressive measure of success in frontier saloons. He even managed to somehow establish himself as a respectable member of western society—until his hell-raising tendencies finally got him cut down in a hail of bullets at a San Antonio theater.

Wild Bill Hickok was one of the most exalted gunfighters ever to roam the West. Not only could he boast of countless near-death experiences with Indians, Confederate soldiers, badmen and black bears, he was also arguably one of the most stylish men in America. Wild Bill loved the camera and showed off his dazzling wardrobe in numerous photographs; writers of the time reciprocated his passion for publicity by weaving florid narratives that ascribed Herculean talents to the handsome frontier killer. Only an untimely demise at the hands of a second-string gunfighter defied the heroic proportions of Hickok's legend.

While most western gunfighters were not endowed with much in the way of moral consistency, "cowboy detective" Charlie Siringo was haunted by his union-busting work for the Pinkerton Detective Agency. Though he often tried to justify his career in his writings by framing his activities as a fight against the forces of anarchy, Siringo's years with the Pinkertons left him a troubled man. Charlie worked as an undercover agent and was a master at infiltrating a group of men, gaining their trust and then betraying them; after 20-some years with the agency, he could not shake the weight of Judas from his conscience. His later years were marked by drawn-out legal battles with the Pinkerton agency over what he could and could not say about his time with the firm. The fact that he would never be able to write a complete, uncensored account of his adventures with the Pinkertons was a serious blow to Siringo, a natural storyteller who had six books published before his death in 1928.

And then there was Bill Doolin. After perfecting the perfidious trade of banditry during his tenure with the notorious Dalton Gang (a story featured in the first volume of this series), Doolin formed his own band soon after the Daltons were wiped out. His Wild Bunch became the scourge of the Oklahoma Territory through much of the 1890s. The gang's numerous heists, lethal encounters and close scrapes with the law made its leader into one of the region's most infamous outlaws. Doolin was finally gunned down in 1896; he would be one of the last of the old-time gunfighters to terrorize the American West.

As succeeding waves of sedentary settlers brought institutions such as schools, churches and families to "civilize" the West, they carved a structured and lawful society out of the untamed, underpopulated wilderness that had allowed the gunfighters to thrive. The closing days of the 19th century also brought about a wave of new technology. Thomas Edison had perfected the duplex telegraph in 1872; by the late 1880s, even the far reaches of the West had been wired. When lawmen were able to telegram neighboring towns or railroad stations to warn of approaching bandits, the element of surprise that allowed for effective mayhem tended to dissipate. After 1900, automobiles, telephones and modern police techniques such as fingerprinting would dramatically improve the efficiency of law enforcement—making old-style outlawry virtually impossible and ending the practice of hiring ruthless killers as peace officers. The outlaws and lawmen whose lives and exploits are chronicled in this book were very much creatures of their time, destined to become extinct as the century drew to a close and the Wild West became the stuff of legend.

FOREWORD

WYATT EARP

1

WYATT EARP

It was said that Wyatt could convey so much contempt with a single glance that it felt as if he were looking straight into your heart and seeing nothing but garbage. Moreover, he could follow up his threatening countenance with deadly action if he so chose.

In the early hours of Sunday, January 13, 1929, as the sun slowly peeked over the vast horizon of the Great Plains, beginning its journey west over the southern Rockies and the scorched earth of the Great Basin, Wyatt Earp lay quietly in his Los Angeles home, his 80-year-old frame unable to bear the weight of its years any longer. While he rested—cared for by his doting wife, pressed in the fresh linen of his sickbed and tended constantly by a doctor and nurse—his thoughts may have drifted back to the turbulent land that he knew as a young man. There, his stern eyes had drifted over the wild territory that whispered of opportunity and adventure to the ambitious spirit. There, his own lust for fortune had led him through some of the roughest regions in the American hinterlands, eventually casting him square in the center of the legendary gunfight at the OK Corral, where he had coolly stared down death as bullets sang and bodies dropped onto the dusty streets of Tombstone, Arizona.

Wyatt Earp lived a long, vigorous life that took him from hunting bison when the Sioux Confederacy ruled the short-grass plains to dealing faro in the smoky, violent saloons that were a fixture of the frontier towns. At different times, he had been a prospector, hunter, saloon manager, stage messenger, railway contractor, outlaw and lawman. If any man can be said to have lived out the romance of the West to its fullest, it was Wyatt Earp.

Yet by and large, posterity has forgotten the wealth of the old adventurer's frontier experience. Wyatt's legend overlooks the greater part of his life, which he spent as a stubbornly hopeful opportunist looking for profit wherever he could find it. His fame, or notoriety, rests instead on the six harsh years when he wore a silver badge in Kansas and the Arizona Territory. During this time, Wyatt Earp became a fearsome six-gun force in two of the most lawless frontier towns the United States ever knew. Commissioned as a peace officer in Dodge City from 1876 to 1879, some of the borough's wildest years, Wyatt established a reputation as a stern lawman whose grip on his composure was as firm as the strength of his convictions. But it was the three following years, spent in Tombstone, Arizona, where Wyatt was pulled into blood-soaked rivalry with the Clanton and McLaury clans, that would secure his place in the annals of American legend.

Wyatt Earp was born in Monmouth, Illinois, on March 19, 1848, the fourth of Nicholas Earp's six sons. Nick Earp himself was the ideal frontier man. Possessed of enough strength of character to serve as a frontier judge, Wyatt's imposing father also made a living as a farmer, cooper, still operator and storekeeper. A restless man by nature, he moved his family frequently as his children grew. A rugged individualist whose highest credo was self-reliance, the industrious patriarch managed to carve a niche for his family wherever he took them.

Wyatt's own sturdy character did not mark him as peculiar among the other men in the Earp family. While the eldest and youngest of the boys, Newton and Warren, did not figure largely in the Earp brothers' exploits, James, Virgil, Wyatt and Morgan all obviously inherited their father's wanderlust and "make-do" practicality, spending much of their lives on western trails on the lookout for opportunity. By the time Wyatt was 20 years of age, he had already lived in Illinois, Iowa, Missouri and California, and had worked as a stage driver, railway spotter, freight hauler and boxing referee.

For a short period, it appears that Wyatt may have considered a sedentary life. In 1870, while living with his brother Newton in Lamar, Missouri, he courted and married Urilla Sutherland, an established young local woman. Quick on the heels of his marriage, Wyatt was given his first job as a lawman, winning the electoral contest for town constable. Who knows what kind of man Wyatt might have become in quiet Lamar if fate had not plotted against him. Shortly after the nuptial blessings, typhoid fever struck down Urilla, widowing Wyatt at the tender age of 22. Disillusioned and directionless in what must have been profound grief, Wyatt turned in his badge and left Missouri for good.

Many accounts describe Wyatt changing dramatically after his wife passed away. He had never been the most gregarious man on the frontier, but upon his leaving Lamar, a dour, foreboding demeanor grew on him like a thick shell. Wyatt Earp rarely smiled, and his steel blue eyes could harden into a look of such disdain that many a fearless desperado trembled under his gaze and thought twice before pushing any contentious issue with the man.

The next few years make up a shady period in Wyatt's history. Soon after leaving Lamar, he drifted into the lawless Indian Territory, where, within months, he was arrested for horse rustling. Wyatt escaped to Kansas before his case was tried, eventually making his living in the buffalo camps by selling hides from the game he had bagged while on the plains and gambling in the rowdy saloons that swallowed up most hunters' hard-earned profits. During these years Earp was a solitary man, given to wandering alone among sprawling herds of buffalo and the dissolute denizens of the buffalo camps. Not given to the pie-eyed revelry that so many of the rootless men of the West were infamous for, Wyatt was never seen to touch a drop of liquor. He kept his thoughts to himself and remained aloof from the violence around him. Nevertheless, he was a regular at the gambling tables and displayed a remarkable intelligence at cards. His success at the monte, faro and poker tables was almost unmatched. Young Bat Masterson, one of the few friends Earp made while hunting buffalo, would later confirm the stories about Wyatt's skill at the tables, claiming that he had never seen a better gambler in action.

The same steady nerves and exact judgment that allowed Wyatt to succeed at the poker table served him well in tense moments of law enforcement. The fact that a successful gambler and an effective lawman sprang from a single character speaks volumes about the nature of justice in the West. When powerful factions struggled for control of towns, businesses and land, they often employed tobacco-chewing, whiskey-guzzling, trash-talking ruffians from the murkiest pools of American society to do their dirty work. So it was that many lawmen of the 19th century were outlaws in neighboring states. Just as the American Gomorrahs bred the worst kind of frontier men, so too did they attract the individuals who knew how to fight lawlessness on its own terms.

Wyatt Earp wandered through some of the worst settlements the West had to offer, slowly building the reputation of a man to be respected. He was not physically imposing; standing a little over six feet and weighing around 150 pounds, Wyatt had a slender build. But it was his stoic seriousness, coupled with his penetrating glare, that caused most adversaries to stop in their tracks. It was said that Wyatt could convey so much contempt with a single glance that it felt as if he were looking straight into your heart and seeing nothing but garbage. Moreover, he could follow up his threatening countenance with deadly action if he so chose. In the regular target matches that took place in the camps, Wyatt proved himself quick and deadly with rifle and pistol, repeatedly demonstrating his superiority over the other marksmen. Thus Wyatt Earp received something of a gunslinger's education while roaming through Kansas in the early 1870s, preparing him for the innumerable confrontations he would eventually face in the toughest towns of the West.

After a brief stint as a policeman in Wichita, Wyatt roamed into Dodge City in the spring of 1876, when the notorious municipality was only four years old. The cattle town was far from innocent in its infancy, having recorded nine homicides during its very first year. And as the herds of longhorns being driven up the Western Trail swelled, they brought ever-increasing numbers of Texan cowpunchers into town. Businesses in Dodge thrived on the wild revelries these Texans enjoyed at trail's end, but with Texan money came Texan violence.

In the 1870s, most of the cowboys working on the range were ex-Confederate soldiers, struggling to survive in the economically devastated Lone Star State. The necessities of the cattle industry seasonally drove thousands of these Civil War veterans into the small Kansan cattle towns with their herds of longhorns. The result was an inevitable stirring up of North-South tensions and still-fresh memories of "Bleeding Kansas," the name given to the era between 1853 and 1861 when hundreds of people died in violence between free-state and pro-slavery factions. As Dodge City came to dominate the livestock trade along the Santa Fe line, it became the liveliest cattle town in Kansas; during the summer months, it was packed full of swaggering, irritable and inebriated cowpunchers who were bent on tomfoolery ranging from harmless stunts to downright deadly mayhem. By the time Wyatt Earp rode into Dodge City, the exploits of these Texans had put about 70 or 80 men on Boot Hill.

Wyatt Earp was appointed as a peace officer in May 1876 and immediately distinguished himself as an effective lawman who was sensitive to the intricacies of his office. The principal crime in Dodge was toting a gun north of the Dead Line, which was drawn at the Santa Fe tracks. The rule was that almost anything went south of the line, but if a man was seen with his guns after he crossed the tracks, that man took his life into his own hands because it gave the law justification to shoot on sight. Unlike enforcers such as Wild Bill Hickok, who reportedly shot first and asked questions later, Wyatt respected the cowboys who brought business into his town, but he still managed to make it clear that there would be zero tolerance for transgression. In the overwhelming majority of his confrontations with cowboys, Wyatt jerked his gun only to "buffalo" the offender—an ugly but effective procedure in western law enforcement that consisted of beating a man's skull with the barrel of a revolver. The next morning, the lawbreaker would wake in the calaboose with a splitting headache and a minor fine, but he'd still be above ground. By consistently manhandling instead of murdering, Wyatt made sure that the city ordinances were enforced, yet did not fuel the animosity of the Texans by creating martyrs.

For example, in the summer of 1877, an arrogant young cattle king by the name of Tobe Driskill roared across the Dead Line with two smoking revolvers, determined to turn Dodge on its ear in celebration of his enormous earnings from that year's drive. He was followed by an enthusiastic group of cowpunchers who strode up and down Front Street emptying their pistols into the air. Driskill paused in front of the Alhambra Saloon, calling down Mayor James Kelley in a profane invitation to discuss who was really running Dodge.

FRONT STREET, DODGE CITY, KANSAS

Then Wyatt Earp appeared. Tearing right down the middle of Front Street, he made a beeline for Driskill with murder in his eyes. Someone shouted a warning to Tobe, but before he could react, Wyatt sent Driskill sprawling into the dirt while almost simultaneously yanking the Texan's revolvers from his hands. Seconds later, the young cattle king was being dragged down Front Street by the scruff of his neck; without so much as a word from Wyatt, Driskill was unceremoniously hurled into the calaboose. In a later interview, Wyatt stated that he wanted to get the message across with this public thrashing that he held Driskill in such low regard that the young man was not even worth drawing against. Only such supreme self-assurance could have dissolved the mob that had gathered that night.

Upon hearing the news of Driskill's imprisonment, Tobe's foreman, a veteran gunfighter, promptly led a group of about 25 armed cowboys across the Dead Line with the intent of freeing his employer. They converged on the prison with their weapons drawn, yelling out taunts at anyone who might dare stop them. One of the men had just begun to work on the lock of the jail with a sledgehammer when, for the second time that night, the solitary figure of Wyatt Earp appeared. This time he walked calmly, guns holstered, through the group of Texans, straight toward the man with the hammer. Casting his glowering stare about the group to find the boss of this band, he finally sized up the foreman.

"Quit pounding on that lock," Wyatt snapped at the man before the door. "You fellows better not start something you can't stop," he continued, this time directly addressing the leader of Driskill's would-be liberators.

The shouts from the gang suddenly ceased, and the cowboy working on the door looked doubtfully at the foreman, who stood gawking nervously at Wyatt. The lone lawman stood before the gathered cowpunchers, staring at their leader as if he were pond scum.

Wyatt broke the silence. "Put up your guns," he snarled, "and get out of town. Before you go, put that sledgehammer back where you got it."

According to legend, Driskill's foreman slowly turned and walked for the Dead Line without a word. He was soon followed by his cowed gang. The next morning, Tobe Driskill was released from jail with a fine of $100.

The lion's share of Wyatt's work in Dodge played out peacefully. Shots were rarely fired and resolutions were almost always quick and clean—more often than not ending with a humiliated Texan nursing his ego in the confines of the Dodge prison. As the number of arrests increased, word spread that Dodge was taking a firm stance against lawlessness and its most active officer was a man by the name of Wyatt Earp.

During his time in Dodge, Wyatt seems to have softened his reclusive shell, fostering friendships that would last through much of his life. Walking the beat during Dodge's raucous summer nights, he planted the seeds of a number of relationships, and he quickly became a regular at the faro tables in the Long Branch and Alhambra saloons. Some historians have speculated that he worked with the Long Branch's famous gambler, Luke Short, rigging games so the odds worked in their favor. Whatever the case, Wyatt and Luke did well at the tables during Dodge's booming summer months and established a friendship that would eventually take them both to the blistering deserts of the Arizona Territory.

Bat Masterson, who had been just a homesick teenager when Wyatt first befriended him on the buffalo range, also made a living in Dodge as a lawman and gambler. Understandably, his friendship with Wyatt solidified under the heat of the trials the two men faced together. Bat often stood squarely with Wyatt in the line of duty, staring down gun-toting ruffians in the streets of the cattle town. In 1881, Bat also worked for a short time in Tombstone, with Wyatt, but not before he achieved impressive success as a lawman in Kansas, serving a term as sheriff of Ford County.

Though Wyatt had an affair with Celia Ann "Mattie" Blaylock, one of Dodge's "soiled doves," his friendship with the notorious John "Doc" Holliday was the strongest bond he forged with anyone during his years in Dodge. Late in 1877, Wyatt was commissioned by the Santa Fe Railroad to hunt down Dave Rudabaugh, a depraved renegade who was robbing the company's pay trains and construction camps.

DOC HOLLIDAY

Rudabaugh's trail led Wyatt into Fort Griffin, Texas, where the fated meeting with Doc Holliday took place. Holliday was reputed to be one of the most cold-blooded men on the frontier. Slowly dying of tuberculosis, he had given up his career as a dentist and taken up the life of a dissolute six-gun gambler with a zeal that few could match. Although his bad nerves and emaciated frame made Doc appear more a man to pity than to fear, when he was moved to violent action his hands suddenly became steady and lightning quick. Holliday could take down any gunslinger who dared draw against him. Likened physically to a walking cadaver, Doc was a twitching mess of hot-tempered meanness that killed without compunction. Yet, if he considered you a friend, his loyalty was unbending. Later on in his life, when Bat Masterson was asked to describe Holliday, he expressed his deep dislike for Doc's "selfish" and "perverse" nature, but nevertheless allowed the man three redeeming traits: his courage, his fervent loyalty to his friends, and his affection for Wyatt Earp.

When they first met, Wyatt Earp and Doc Holliday were not overly amiable with each other, but the strength of their personalities eventually overcame the force of their circumstances until respected lawman and detested outlaw became steadfast friends. Holliday rode into Dodge early in the summer of 1878 to visit Wyatt and enjoy the entertainment the town had to offer. Little did he know then that his friendship with the town's deputy marshal would inadvertently put his guns on the side of the law.

On September 24 of that year, about 20 cowboys led by Ed Morrison and Tobe Driskill (the same Tobe Driskill whom Wyatt had embarrassed the year before) rode into Dodge intent on raising Cain. Under the impression that Wyatt was not in town, the boys galloped down Front Street, shooting out windows and whooping in drunken glee. They headed for the Long Branch Saloon, determined to smash up what they saw as Wyatt's unofficial headquarters. Wyatt was on the northeast edge of town when the cowboys began their rampage; upon hearing the opening shots of the riot, he quickly headed for the Long Branch to get at the shotguns he had stashed there. He had miscalculated the location of the Texans, however, and as he turned onto Front Street, right before the Long Branch itself, he suddenly found himself face to face with the drunken cowboys. Their guns were drawn and their intentions wicked.

"By God," Driskill bellowed, "it's Earp!"

Ed Morrison looked hard through a drunken fog before his eyes confirmed what Driskill had just exclaimed. "You son of a bitch," Morrison growled, "I've waited years for this! Your time has come!"

Wyatt stood before the mob, his hands hovering over the handles of his Colt Peacemakers. Looking at the angry faces of the men before him, half of whom he had probably manhandled at one time or another, Wyatt found himself reluctantly agreeing with Morrison's avowal. It did seem that Earp's time had truly come. As 20 vicious men trained their guns on Wyatt, the young lawman's mind raced through his options, but every scenario seemed to end with his own imminent demise.

Morrison pulled back the hammers of his pistols. "Pray, you son of a bitch," he snarled, "or jerk your gun and–"

He was never able to finish his threat. The doors of the Long Branch burst open and the ashen figure of Doc Holliday leapt out into the night. Both of his guns were drawn and cocked, one aimed right at Morrison's head. Something like a grin distorted Doc's pale face.

"Throw 'em up!" Doc ordered. "Throw 'em up, you murdering cow thieves!"

Doc had been playing cards in the back of the Long Branch when the boys began shooting up the town. Not the kind of man to interrupt a serious poker game on account of a little gunfire, Holliday had barely acknowledged the ruckus outside. But his attitude had suddenly changed when what was transpiring between Wyatt and the cowboys became obvious to everyone in the saloon. With a sudden lurch, Doc had rushed from the poker table to the pistol rack at the end of the bar and jumped out the door.

The cowboys were distracted for an instant by the sight of one of the most feared gunfighters on the frontier leering at them from the doorway of the Long Branch. This was all the time Wyatt needed. In the blink of an eye, he skinned his Peacemakers—and suddenly the cowboys found themselves covered under four pistols wielded by the two sharpest shooters in Dodge City. While the odds were still stacked in the cowboys' favor, the notion that at least four of them were guaranteed plots on Boot Hill did much to deflate their enthusiasm. Furthermore, the direction of the muzzles of Earp's and Holliday's guns made Morrison and Driskill painfully aware that they would be the first to go down if a shoot-out commenced. The leaders of the little insurrection rapidly became the least interested in its continuation.

Sensing the sudden loss of resolve in the Texans' ranks, Doc broke the silence with his thick Southern drawl. "What'll we do with 'em, Wyatt?"

Wyatt responded by walking straight up to Ed Morrison and buffaloing the man where he stood. As the fearsome cowpuncher crumpled to the ground, Wyatt roared at the rest of the gang, "Throw 'em up! All the way and empty! You, Driskill! You're next!"

At once, all of the cowboys dropped their weapons and reached for the sky—all, that is, except for one young man in the rear of the pack who kept his revolver trained on Wyatt. Holliday shouted a warning to his friend as two shots split the air, one a half-second before the other. Holliday had fired first, sending a slug tearing through the shoulder of the aspiring assassin. While the cowboy was only an instant behind Doc in firing, it was enough time for Doc's bullet to cover the distance and blast the cowboy's aim off the intended target.

Later on that evening, Doc and Wyatt, outlaw and lawman, were seen marching the browbeaten cowboys down Front Street and into prison. Fines were issued the next morning.

The suppression of the Driskill–Morrison raid was the last serious confrontation that Wyatt would have with cowboys in Dodge. By the following year, the volume of cattle trade in town had diminished considerably, so Wyatt spent most of his time dealing at the faro and monte tables in the Long Branch. Quickly growing restless in the subdued atmosphere, Wyatt and his brother James, who was bartending in Dodge at that time, were attracted to the promise of opportunity in a newly formed mining town in the Arizona Territory. The name of the town was Tombstone. Recently discovered silver in the surrounding San Pedro Hills sent the population of the borough soaring from zero in 1879 to 5600 in 1881. With such rampant growth came great potential for profit–and profit was the premier tenet of the Earp boys' faith. Wyatt and Jim left Dodge late in 1879, visions of fortune foremost on their minds. Joining up with their brother Virgil, they arrived in Tombstone in December of that year.

The industrious Earp boys did not waste any time. Jim, Virgil and Wyatt acquired shares in numerous speculative ventures, staking interests in mining claims, town lots and water and timber rights. Jim soon got work as a bartender in a local saloon, Virgil attained a commission as a deputy U.S. marshal and Wyatt got an administrative position as deputy sheriff. He also bought a share in the mining camp's busiest establishment, the Oriental Saloon. Early in 1880, a fourth Earp rode into town. Hot-tempered Morgan, the youngest of the four in Tombstone, got work riding shotgun for Wells Fargo. Though every indication suggests that the Earp brothers came to Tombstone solely as fortune hunters, the forces at work in the booming mining camp inexorably drew them into conflict with the powerful cowboy faction that ruled the surrounding countryside.

The cowboys, led by the Clanton and McLaury clans, had been raising and rustling cattle along the San Pedro River long before the town of Tombstone was born. These boys were the same kind of men Wyatt had battled in Dodge: They were a hard-riding, hell-raising band of toughs, and their early settlement of the region had emboldened them against the recently arrived inhabitants of Tombstone. When coming into town to sell their livestock, they often lingered on for days, shamelessly terrorizing the town with drunken crime sprees and flying lead. It must have been difficult for Wyatt to stand passively by, curbing the instincts that had driven him during his years in Dodge; but for a short while at least, he managed to remain aloof from the violence that plagued Tombstone.

But fate had other plans, and before long the Earps found themselves drawn into a tense rivalry with the cowboys. It started not a year after the brothers had settled in town. In October 1880, one of the cowboys' most sadistic riders, a murderer by the name of Curly Bill Brocius, shot Tombstone's marshal, Fred White, while on a bender. It was then that the patience of the Earps finally broke. Right after the shooting, in a short, bloodless confrontation on Allen Street, they apprehended Curly Bill and dispersed his confederates. Curly Bill was released from prison shortly thereafter as a result of White's mysterious deathbed testimony that the desperado had shot him by accident.

Motivated either by base opportunism or an awakened sense of duty, Virgil Earp assumed the deadly office of town marshal upon White's death, and thereby drew the Earp brothers into the crooked politics of Tombstone. In his efforts to enforce law in the wild borough, Virgil was soon confounded by the cowboys' connection to a powerful political force in the area. Johnny Behan, the town's leading Democrat, worked in close association with the rogues, counting on their rough influence over the region for his own political and economic success. In exchange for the muscle the cowboys lent to the Democratic ring that controlled the region, Behan turned a blind eye to their cattle rustling and stagecoach robbery.

While Behan's connections with these men did nothing to endear him to the Earps, Behan himself grew to hate Wyatt for the attention that his mistress, the beautiful Josephine Sarah Marcus, gave the itinerant lawman. The two men soon found expression for their mutual enmity in the political rivalry that developed between them. In February 1881, after double-crossing Wyatt in a tenuous political alliance they had formed, Behan was appointed sheriff of the newly formed Cochise County. Wyatt was not the kind of man who took defeat easily, and he became determined to win the county seat in the next round of elections.

These were elections that Wyatt would never see; before the year was over, the Earps' tensions with the cowboy faction would erupt into full-out war. And unlike Wyatt's previous dealings with rogue cowboys, the battles with these cowpunchers would not leave him untouched. Whatever protector had hovered over the lawman's shoulder in Dodge demanded a heavy toll for its services in Tombstone. Over the next year and a half, a whirlwind of violence tore through Tombstone, leaving one brother dead, one crippled–and one left to exact the ugly duty of vengeance.

Behan was not the only man in Tombstone who kept unpleasant company. From the very start, Wyatt's ambitions for the county seat were threatened by the type of men with whom he associated. As if it were not bad enough that the infamous Doc Holliday had followed the Earps into town and was often seen in the company of the prospective sheriff, Wyatt's old gambling buddy Luke Short had been forced to flee Tombstone less than two months after he was hired on at the Oriental Saloon. Short had shot a man in a gambling dispute just after Behan's appointment to the county seat in 1881. So when three bandits killed a couple of Kinnear & Company employees during a botched stage robbery in March of that same year, Wyatt rode out to prove himself and win the confidence of Cochise County. He believed the manhunt would make or break his bid as sheriff.

The posse met with limited success. After two weeks in the saddle pursuing the bandits, Wyatt, Virgil and Morgan rode back into Tombstone, weary, dusty and empty-handed. Despite being thwarted by a fruitless chase, Wyatt did not give up. His single-minded ambition drove him to strike a clandestine bargain with a sworn enemy of the Earps–Ike Clanton, the loudest and most unruly of the Clanton brothers and a notorious member of the Cochise County cowboys. The stage robbers had evaded his posse, so Wyatt secretly offered Ike the reward money on the outlaws' heads if he would rat them out. The greedy cowpuncher liked the idea and revealed the location of the bandits' hideout to Wyatt. The two men's scheme was ultimately confounded, however, when the robbers were killed during a failed heist in New Mexico before Wyatt could arrest them.

In the stifling summer heat of 1881, tension between the Earps and the cowboys was mounting. The town split into two blocs. The Earp faction was a Republican business interest based in Tombstone, and the cowboy group was backed by Behan and other Democrats. Accusations flew. In June, Doc Holliday was arrested as one of the suspects in the stage robbery in March. Though he was soon acquitted, rumors quickly spread that the Earps themselves were felons and that they were responsible for the sudden increase in stage robberies during that summer. In response, the Earps pointed out the criminal operations of the cowboys and accused Behan's office of working with the bandits in their cattle rustling and stage robbing. As relations turned from sour to rotten, Ike Clanton festered under the accusations of his own conscience. Constantly terrified that Wyatt might spread word of his treachery earlier that spring to the other cowboys, Ike affected an extreme hatred of the Earps and brashly denounced them whenever he had an audience. On the evening of October 25, 1881, his tough talk finally caught up with him.

Ike was on an all-night drinking binge, stumbling through the saloons of Tombstone and swilling whiskey like it was water. By the time he wandered into the Alhambra Saloon, half the town had heard what he would do to Holliday and any one of the Earp brothers if he got the chance. Though Morgan and Wyatt were in the Alhambra when Ike lurched in, the pie-eyed cowboy did not notice them, and the Earp brothers seemed intent on avoiding a conflict that night. The mood in the Alhambra changed, however, when Doc sauntered in a

TOMBSTONE, ARIZONA TERRITORY, 1881

few minutes later. A different breed of man than the Earps, Holliday was not the sort to let threats go unanswered.

Upon seeing Ike, Doc walked without hesitation to where the drunken cowboy was sitting and, in a voice strained with anger, muttered, "You cowboy son of a bitch, get out your guns and get to work."

Ike looked up at Doc standing there like death itself and whimpered, "I don't have any guns."

As Doc began shouting insults at the shrinking Ike, Wyatt advised Morgan—who was on duty as policeman that night—that he best separate the men before someone got hurt. Morgan walked up to the table, took Doc's arm and pulled him out onto the street.

Morgan had probably saved Ike's life inside the Alhambra, but the cowpuncher walked away insulted and fueled his grudge with generous doses of whiskey for the rest

of the night. By 11 AM on October 26, he was in a drunken rage. Walking through the streets of Tombstone waving a rifle and a six-shooter, he was heard hollering, "As soon as those damned Earps show their faces on the street today, the ball will commence."

He did not have to wait long. Virgil, then acting marshal of Tombstone, spotted Ike in an alley and moved quickly to arrest him. The elder Earp calmly walked up to Ike from behind and almost casually yanked the rifle from Ike's hands. Spinning around and going for his six-shooter, Ike was not quick enough to stop the barrel of Virgil's Peacemaker from crashing over his head.

Virgil looked down at the prone outlaw and softly asked, "You been hunting for me?"

"If I'd seen you a second sooner, I'd have killed you," Ike spat back.

With his weapon still drawn, Virgil arrested Ike for carrying guns within city limits. Along with Morgan, who had just arrived as Ike was buffaloed, Tombstone's marshal marched the cowboy to the county's justice of the peace.

All hell broke loose at the courthouse. Wyatt, fed up with the threats and controversy that had been dragging on through the whole summer, strode into court with his guns loosened in his holsters, eager for some kind of resolution.

Hot words were exchanged between Ike and Wyatt and—perhaps to prevent a murder in the courtroom—Wyatt stormed out before too much was said. Outside, he found himself face to face with Tom McLaury, who was just arriving to check on Ike. Tom was not one of the cowboys' best gunfighters, but nevertheless he was not at all afraid of Wyatt. Still steaming from the exchange with Ike, Wyatt unleashed a string of expletives.

"If you want to make a fight, I'll make a fight with you anywhere," the cowboy responded.

At this, Wyatt jerked out his six-shooter with lightning speed and buffaloed Tom where he stood. As McLaury's eyes glazed over and he fell onto the street, Wyatt stormed away from the courthouse without so much as a look back.

Ike paid his fine and walked out of the courthouse that same morning, still drunk. The beating he had taken at the hands of Virgil Earp added to the humiliation he had suffered in the Alhambra. Instead of leaving Tombstone, he dawdled around town with his brother Billy Clanton and Frank McLaury. Tom McLaury soon joined them, rubbing his scalp. Incensed by the insults they had suffered that morning, the cowboys carried their guns openly, strutting up and down the streets of Tombstone, loudly hurling insults at the whole Earp clan. Before long, they settled in an empty lot near the OK Corral, where Ike's drinking binge of the night before began to take its toll on him under the hot midday sun.

The Earp brothers were gathered not two blocks away, steeling themselves for the conflict that was now inevitable. Virgil was marshal, and these cowboys were breaking the law. They had to be disarmed. When Behan got wind of the impending confrontation, he approached the cowboys alone and tried to talk them into dropping their guns.

"Not unless you disarm the Earps," snapped Frank McLaury, one of the cowboys' sharpest gunmen.

By this time, the Earp brothers had started down Fourth Street, walking toward the OK Corral with calm deliberation. Doc Holliday, draped in a long overcoat and leaning heavily on a cane, stopped them in the middle of the street. His pale skin was glistening with a feverish sweat.

The tubercular gunman rasped, "Where are you headed, Wyatt?"

"Down the street to make a fight."

"About time," Doc replied. He looked down Fourth Street, lost in thought for a moment. "Mind if I tag along?"

Wyatt glanced at Virgil, who, as town marshal, was probably wary of associating with a character like Holliday. "This is our fight," Wyatt responded. "There's no call for you to mix in."

"That's a hell of a thing for you to say to me," Holliday coughed back, offended that his only friend on earth would think of going into a gunfight without him.

Wyatt looked from Virgil to Doc before replying, "All right."

Virgil deputized Doc right there in the middle of Fourth Street, trading the shotgun he carried for Doc's cane. The marshal's advice to his new deputy was short and to the point: "Hide that shotgun under your coat where it won't attract so much attention."

Walking four abreast, Wyatt, Morgan, Virgil and Doc turned the corner onto Fremont Street and headed into what would become the most famous gunfight in the history of the West.

OK CORRAL

As they approached the lot where the cowboys were gathered, Behan came running up to the foursome. "Earp," he blurted, addressing Virgil, "for God's sake, don't go down there!"

"I'm going to disarm them," Virgil snapped back. Without breaking their stride, the Earps and Holliday brushed by the panicked sheriff.

In desperation, Behan yelled at their backs, "Go back! I am sheriff of this county!" But the determined men gave no indication of even hearing him. Walking into the empty lot that was enclosed by a photograph gallery on one end and William Harwood's home on the other, the four gunfighters suddenly found themselves no more than six feet from the cowboys, who stood with their backs against Harwood's home.

At first, there was only silence. The Earps blocked the front of the lot; there was no place to take cover. The tension in the air made it obvious that neither negotiation nor insult had any place in the 20-foot-wide stretch of ground. Virgil stood in front, with Doc's cane in his hand, Wyatt and Morgan were behind him, and Doc was in the rear, his fluttering greatcoat revealing the shotgun he held underneath.

Virgil interrupted the heavy silence. "Throw up your hands!" the town marshal barked.

Frank McLaury and Billy Clanton responded by pulling back the hammers of their holstered Colts. The sound of the cocked hammers sent the Earps' hands to their holsters; Doc's coat fell into the dust as he raised his shotgun to his shoulder. Virgil's next words rang weakly against the rising current of inevitable violence: "Hold! I want your guns."

Someone answered, "Son of a bitch," but was not able to finish. The tension finally broke; guns were drawn, hammers were cocked and bullets would do the rest of the talking for the next blood-soaked minute. Billy Clanton and Wyatt Earp were the first to get shots off. Billy jerked his pistol and aimed at Wyatt, who ignored him and shot instead at Frank McLaury, whom he recognized as the best gunfighter among this group of cowboys. Billy missed, his round tearing through the skirt of Wyatt's coat, but Frank was blown back on his heels, shot through the stomach. Doubled over, one hand over his gut, Frank staggered towards Fremont Street. In the following instant, Tom McLaury leapt behind his brother's horse, reaching for the rifle that was holstered in the saddle.

Billy Clanton was hit next. After the cowboy missed Wyatt for the third time, Morgan fired twice at him. Billy was thrown against Harwood's home as one bullet smashed through his right wrist and the other lodged in his chest. But he was not out of the fight yet; as he slumped to ground, he switched his pistol into his left hand and continued to fire on his assailants. At this point, Ike lost his stomach for the fight and ran towards Wyatt, grabbing Earp's arm in mortal panic and crying, "Don't kill me, Wyatt! Don't kill me! I'm not shooting!"

Wyatt coolly threw him off, answering, "The fight's commenced. Get to fighting or get out."

Even before Ike's trembling legs took him out of the action, Doc emptied one of the barrels of his shotgun into the air, sending Frank's spooked horse galloping onto Fremont Street. The next instant found Tom McLaury standing in the open, staring into the depraved eyes of Doc Holliday. The second time Doc's shotgun roared, buckshot tore through the right side of McLaury's chest, sending him stumbling down Fremont Street, where he crumpled onto the dirt to die.

For an instant, it must have seemed like the battle was over. Three of the cowboys were badly wounded and the fourth had run off. But the will to fight had not been driven out of the rogues just yet. Billy Clanton, slumped against Harwood's home, steadied his wobbly revolver by bracing it over his right arm and singled out Virgil in the melee. The marshal yelled out as Billy's bullet tore though his calf and he was blown off his feet. Out on Fremont Street, Frank McLaury turned to the man who had just killed his brother. Growling through blood-drenched teeth, the dying cowboy snarled at Holliday, "I have you now, you son of a bitch."

"Blaze away," taunted Holliday. "You're a daisy if you do."

Three shots sounded simultaneously. Frank's shot went through Holliday's hip as Morgan's and Doc's rounds struck Frank below the ear and through the heart. The cowpuncher was dead before he hit the ground.

The only cowboy left was Billy Clanton, and he fired his last shot at Morgan as he struggled to get to his feet. Morgan fell as the bullet pierced his shoulder, but he still managed to answer Billy's report. He and Wyatt fired simultaneously, throwing Billy back onto the ground with two more bullets buried below his ribs. Clanton lay there, still trying to cock his empty revolver in the last moments of his life.

The gunfight was over in under a minute. With three men dead and three men wounded, the legendary shoot-out did nothing to resolve the feud that plagued the town. In fact, the effect of the three dead cowboys on the mood of the county must have reminded Wyatt why he had never fired his gun as a peace officer in Dodge. The power of martyrs is always considerable. Billy Clanton and Tom and Frank McLaury reached beyond the grave, adding the fire of vengeance to the struggle between the Earps and the cowboys.

As the Earps' supporters armed themselves to protect the brothers and their families from retaliation, a grand funeral was held for the slain men. It drew an enormous procession of mourners, and the Earps soon discovered that their popularity was waning. Sheriff Behan imprisoned Doc and Wyatt for murder. After 30 days of testimony, Judge Wells Spicer acquitted the two friends, stating that they were acting in the interests of the law by "disarming brave and determined men...who had previously declared their intentions not to be disarmed." Nevertheless, the judge still dismissed Virgil from the position of town marshal, ruling that the eldest Earp had "committed an injudicious and censurable act" by deputizing Doc and Wyatt before confronting the McLaurys and Clantons.

In the eyes of the cowboys, the law had failed to bring the Earps to justice. So, in the grand tradition of the West, they took the law into their own hands. Barely two months after the shoot-out, the sound of five shotgun reports tore through the streets of Tombstone just before midnight. Minutes later, a terribly wounded, glassy-eyed Virgil Earp stumbled into the bustle of the Oriental Saloon and fell into Wyatt's arms. Two shotgun blasts had found their mark; one had shattered Virgil's left arm and the other had torn a hole through his side. Though Virgil survived, the buckshot blast had destroyed his arm, rendering it useless for the rest of his days. There were no witnesses to the attack.

The worst was to come three months after Virgil's shooting. On a Saturday night in March 1882, Wyatt and Morgan were playing billiards in Bob Hatch's pool hall on Allen Street when two shots shattered the glass in the back door. Amid the screams of patrons diving for cover, young Morgan collapsed. A single bullet had shattered his spine. As he lay dying in Wyatt's arms, he looked at his big brother's grief-stricken face and gasped, "This is the last game of pool I'll ever play." He was dead within the hour.

This time, witnesses identified three men running from the scene of Morgan's murder: Frank Stilwell, who was Sheriff Behan's deputy; a friend of the Clantons by the name of Pete Spence; and Florenzo Cruz, a Mexican whose alias was Indian Charlie. Now it was Wyatt's turn to seek vengeance, and he did so with fervor. Wearing the badge of a deputy U.S. marshal, Wyatt formed a posse around Doc

Holliday and himself, and they tore through the Pima and Cochise counties like a lead-spitting cyclone.

The first to fall was Frank Stilwell, who was shot dead in the train station at Tucson. As Virgil and the Earp women were leaving the Arizona Territory for good, Stilwell and some cowboys had come to the rail yard, hoping to finish off the rest of the Earp clan. Wyatt, however, got the jump on them. Stilwell's body was found the next morning with his clothes covered in powder burns and his body riddled with six bullet holes.

Indian Charlie was next—after he was found hiding at Pete Spence's ranch, Wyatt forced him to draw on the count of three. Earp's mangled Spanish was the last thing Cruz would hear; an instant after the enraged Wyatt barked "tres," three bullets tore through the Mexican gunman's body. The unlucky assassin was not even able to draw his revolver. Pete Spence escaped Wyatt's wrath, but another man would fall before Wyatt's vendetta came to a close.

Behan deputized a group of cowboys to stop Wyatt's killing spree. So it was that one group of lawmen rode out to hunt down another. Tombstone had become a confusion of badges: The law was hunting down the law, no one was innocent and the only thing that was certain was more murder.

Behan's posse was led by the infamous Curly Bill Brocius, one of the cowboys' most feared gunslingers. He met his end at a shoot-out that erupted when the two posses came across each other at Iron Springs. After a short exchange, Wyatt cut the murdering cowboy in half with two barrels of buckshot through the stomach. Though its leader was slain, Behan's posse outnumbered Wyatt's and still managed to drive Earp's boys off. Upon hearing of the battle at Iron Springs, Behan deputized yet another group of cowboys under the homicidal Johnny Ringo. Now even Wyatt and Doc had to admit that they were outgunned. They gave up hope of taking down the last remaining assassin and headed north for Colorado, all branded as wanted men in the Arizona Territory. It would be more than 20 years before Wyatt would return to Arizona.

Wyatt Earp gave up on law enforcement after the bloodshed in Tombstone. He married Behan's ex-mistress, Josephine Sarah Marcus, and spent the rest of his days traveling through western states and dabbling in numerous business ventures. Though he never found much success in these endeavors, Wyatt was unwilling to market his most valuable asset—his life story. Questioned about the happenings in Tombstone for much of his life, Wyatt remained obstinately silent, unwilling to discuss the violence that permanently scarred the Earp name. Indeed, only when he was well into his later years and hungry writers were preying on the tale of his life and producing narratives that outraged him and his wife did Wyatt entertain the idea of telling the story of Tombstone as he saw it. Yet Wyatt would never see a biography that would satisfy him. Dying peacefully, his story never told, Wyatt left behind a legend that would be recreated countless times on the screen and on the written page. Though the many versions of his tale differ on numerous accounts, the legend of Wyatt Earp has always held a special place in popular history. His fame is no surprise; the struggle and strife of Wyatt Earp's days captured the spirit of the lawlessness and stubborn individuality that so often afflicted—and defined—life in the American West.

2

BILL LONGLEY

Bill's narrow brush with death did nothing to deter him from killing others. Spending the next three years as a farmer, cowboy, packmaster, saloonkeeper and gambler, the young man supplemented whatever trade he plied with murder.

A hot wind blew over the prairies of eastern Texas on October 11, 1878. In Lee County, just outside the town of Giddings, an all-too-familiar frontier scene was being played out with morbid determination as thousands of citizens gathered to watch a man hang. The condemned outlaw stood before the mass of people; his bound hands held a lit cigar, and he addressed the crowd before him in a slow, heavy voice:

> If I have any friends here, I hope they will do nothing to avenge my death. If they want to avenge my death, let them pray for me. I deserve this fate. It is a debt I owe for my wild reckless life. When it is paid, it will all be over. I hope you will forgive me. I forgive you…Goodbye, everybody.

BILL BURROWS, BILL LONGLEY AND SHERIFF MAST, 1878

Silence descended on the crowd after the dark-eyed man at the gallows finished his speech. The bright midday sun beat down upon the hangman's scaffold, and for a moment no one made a sound. Then, somewhere among the rough frontier crowd that had gathered for the hanging that day, someone laughed. One or two individuals called out, "Goodbye, Bill!" but the tone of these few farewells was tinged with a bit too much enthusiasm to suggest any kind of sorrow. There was more laughter.

As Bill Longley took a long draw on his last cigar, he looked out at the throng of more than 4000 people that had come to watch him die. What he saw in the impatient faces must have confirmed his lifelong credo, namely, that no one who drew breath could be counted on and a man's guns were his only allies in the world. Grinding his cigar into the gallows' planks, he turned to the group of lawmen who were guarding the platform and muttered, "I see a good many enemies around me and mighty few friends."

Did Longley expect something more after his repentant speech to the citizens of Lee County? Could he really have imagined that there would be a wave of sudden compassion for a hardened killer? A last-minute pardon from a kindhearted governor? Divine intervention from a merciful God? Whatever hopes his deranged mind may have dreamed up during his month of imprisonment were extinguished when the rough twine of the hangman's noose was tightened around his neck. Maybe then he realized that his much-publicized reformation over the previous month did not amount to spit according to the code of Western justice. And Longley's sudden faith in the righteous path did little to temper Texans' memories of his 11-year killing spree.

Reputed to have killed 32 men in his 27 years of life, Bill Longley had a natural talent for murder that was cultivated in the brutish misery of Reconstruction Texas. In the years following the Civil War, from 1866 to 1874, the Lone

Star State was made to swallow the bitter pill of defeat by radical Republicans in Washington. Brought under martial law and carpetbagger rule, many conservative Texans understood Northern "Reconstruction" to be a euphemism for Southern dissolution. As the often-corrupt carpetbagger authorities caused mounting public debt and popular discontent, a new kind of lawlessness began to thrive. The renegades who challenged the unpopular authority of the Reconstruction government earned a distinguished place among Texan outlaws. To many, the murderous careers of gunfighters such as John Wesley Hardin and Bill Longley were something more than homicidal fits thrown by mentally disturbed loners; some raconteurs spun these killers' violence out into legacies of proud Texan resistance to Northern rule in order to preserve what was left of Southern pride after the Civil War.

But Reconstruction malaise only goes so far in explaining Bill Longley's profound meanness. Certainly former slaves and Union soldiers were among the lone gunman's favorite victims, but the stories of Longley's wanderings suggest that he was driven by forces that ran deeper than sectional politics. An avowed misanthrope, Bill Longley was afflicted with a deeply troubled psychology rife with anger and inner contradictions. Hunted by the law and tormented by the mysterious specters of mental illness, Longley spent long periods of time in isolation in the wilderness. Among the scrub oaks and tumbleweeds of Texas, he developed such an egocentric outlook on the world around him that he became incapable of sympathy for anyone or anything but himself.

Whether Bill Longley's cruelty was guided more by political enmity or inherent psychopathic tendencies is unclear. What is certain, however, is that the Texan gunslinger started killing early on in his life, establishing himself as one of the first desperadoes to terrorize the frontier.

It was in 1867–before his 16th birthday–that Bill killed his first man. A black Reconstruction soldier was riding up the Camino Real, drunk and ornery as hell. As he passed through Longley's hometown of Evergreen, the ill-fated soldier threw curses at the whites in his path, gesturing menacingly with his rifle. One of the men who got in the soldier's way was old Campbell Longley, Bill's father. The bluecoat's oaths were cut off by a stern voice from the middle of the road.

"Hey, you good-for-nothing black scalawag, watch who you're talking to, and quit waving that gun around."

The soldier wheeled his horse around and raised his rifle to confront his challenger, but he barely had a chance to register surprise at the sight of the skinny youth who stood there before the youngster drew his pistol and drilled a bullet into the center of the soldier's forehead. As the Union soldier tumbled from his mount, a lanky Bill Longley stood on Evergreen's main street, twirling his Confederate-issue revolver back into its holster while the muzzle was still smoking. His face betrayed no emotion.

Far from being punished for the murder, Bill became something of a hero among the white farmers in Evergreen, and from that day forward, he took a special interest in murdering former slaves. Riding into Lexington, Texas, later that same year, Bill Longley expressed his frustrations over a lost horse race by emptying his pistol into a street party in a black neighborhood. By the time Longley galloped out of town, two men were dead and six were wounded.

Over the next year, Bill spent his time working on his father's farm by day and riding out to look for trouble in and around Evergreen at night. He had soon earned a reputation as a quick-drawing crack shot who hated the recently emancipated black population with a deadly passion. He killed two more men in 1868, and by the time the law chased Longley out of Evergreen in December, he had earned the nickname

"Wild Bill" among citizens who saw the cold-blooded killer as a champion of Southern society. He was 17 years old.

Riding out of Evergreen, Bill found himself alone for the first time in his life. He wandered aimlessly through the backwoods of Texas. Drifting southwest toward San Antonio, Longley rode into Yorktown early in 1869, just as the Sutton–Taylor feud was starting to heat up. Walking his horse down Main Street, the dusty young gunfighter drew many suspicious looks. Perhaps his sins in Evergreen had etched the indelible mark of murder on his countenance, so that all men of his stripe recognized his nature by a mere glance. Maybe the human instinct of self-preservation warned the other men that a predator was in their midst. Whatever the case, young Bill Longley had not been in town an hour when a group of Union soldiers approached him, mistaking him for Charles Taylor, a feared Confederate gunslinger of the Taylor clan who was wanted for horse theft. Given the murder charges on his head in Evergreen, Longley did not bother stating his true identity. He wheeled his horse around and galloped away through the crowded street, but soon found himself in a desperate gun battle on horseback. Turning his six-shooter against white men for the first time, Longley left one of the soldiers dying with a bullet through the gut during an exchange of gunfire just outside of town.

While heading north from Yorktown, Bill may have begun to mull over his place in the world. He had been chased out of his hometown for murder. He had shot down another man within hours of arriving in another borough. The dark prospect of a solitary life on the lam must have loomed large in the young man's mind. It was at this time that he got the idea of joining Cullen Baker's infamous band of marauders. Maybe he reasoned that he would find his place among Baker's depraved bandits—men who had no qualms about robbing local farmers, murdering indiscriminately and living perpetually on the dodge. He spent the next few months near the Texas–Arkansas border, camping out in creek bottoms and oak flats, keeping one ear to the ground for word on where Baker's bandits were riding.

While looking for Baker, Longley met a local horse rustler who was on the run. Though their friendship was surely a tight-lipped one, they must have found some common ground, because they camped together for nearly a month before Bill resumed his crazed waltz with death.

The sun was setting on a hot summer's day when a vicious group of cowboys got the drop on the two wanted men. Bill's new friend had apparently stolen from a few local ranchers, and the vigilantes that had ridden up on the two men were out to exact severe justice for the theft. Assuming Longley to be an accomplice of the horse rustler, the vigilantes beat the two men at gunpoint and unceremoniously strung them up from an oak limb. It was to be the first of several times that Bill was hanged.

Longley and his friend were left convulsing under the oak tree as the vigilantes galloped off. Bill would have become no more than a decomposed corpse hanging by a grotesquely lengthened neck if good fortune had not intervened. How many men would have been spared a premature end at Wild Bill Longley's hands if the next fateful action had not occurred?

Just as the band was cresting a ridge, one of the cowboys turned and emptied his revolver in the direction of the dangling figures. A bullet grazed the rope around Longley's neck and he fell, coughing and wheezing in an agonized sprawl under the oak tree. By the time Bill got his bearings, however, the horse rustler was dead.

Surviving his first hanging with an ugly scar stretched across his neck earned Longley a certain fame among Baker's boys for the six months he rode with them. While very little has been recorded of Longley's stint with the outlaw gang, legend has it that during a raid on the Arkansas border, Bill recognized one of the cowboys who had strung him up earlier that year. Longley escorted the man to the same oak tree that he was hanged under—and hanged the hapless man right back. Just to be fair, Bill also emptied his revolver at the dangling man as he rode off, but unlike the shots fired at the first hanging, Longley's bullets found their mark.

Bill's narrow brush with death did nothing to deter him from killing others. Spending the next three years as a farmer, cowboy, packmaster, saloonkeeper and gambler, the young man supplemented whatever trade he plied with murder. He killed his trail boss while driving a cattle herd through the Indian Territory. He murdered the army quartermaster he worked under when the unfortunate man got wind of Bill's money-making scheme. He killed a man after a gambling dispute in Parkersville, Kansas. More often than not, Bill Longley's abrupt career changes followed someone's death.

And then there was Longley's blind hatred for black men. Intermittently returning to Evergreen between stints of work, he inevitably took up his old habits, picking cotton on his father's farm and terrorizing any dark-skinned man he came across. In 1869 alone, he was reported to have killed eight black men in his hometown.

Indeed, of all the gunfighters in Reconstruction Texas, only John Wesley Hardin was in the same league as Bill Longley. The similarities between the two were the subject of much discussion among Texans. Born within two years of each other, both men were teenagers when they started killing. Heavily influenced by Reconstruction, Hardin and Longley were also both rabidly racist and killed ex-slaves with fervent enthusiasm. Hardin came from a privileged background while Longley's ancestors were humble farmers, but both men were endowed with the same steady nerves and an almost freakish calm in the face of impending violence, and both exhibited the same self-assured arrogance when among other men. Both killed without compunction.

And yet the two men hated each other. Years later, writing from inside the Glavestone jail in 1877, Longley expressed outrage at Hardin's arrogant response to an Austin reporter who had asked him if he ever associated with Bill Longley. Hardin had replied, "I have never had anything to do with the likes of Bill Longley, nor any other such characters, for I only associate with gentlemen of honor." Longley was already upset that he had been sentenced to hang for his crimes while Hardin had received a relatively lenient 25-year sentence, but when Hardin dressed his murderous tendencies in the trappings of a "gentleman of honor," Longley was furious. In a letter to one of his few friends, Captain Milton Mast, Bill revealed a surprising frankness about his crimes:

> Well, I do not propose to boast of being brave at all, but I have had no help in my meanness when it came to killing a man. I have done such things on my own account and always alone, and I am not trying to justify myself in the least, but I do not think that as far as Wes Hardin is concerned in the matter of honor, that neither Hardin nor myself are overburdened.

The mutual enmity between the two gunfighters stemmed from their tense meeting in Evergreen during the fall of 1870. Longley was only 19 years old then, and Hardin 17, but both boys had already earned considerable reputations as deadly gunslingers. The whole town of Evergreen held its breath when it became known that young Wes Hardin had ridden into town to do some gambling. Speculation abounded over what would happen when the killers met. The citizens of Evergreen did not have to wait long for the answer.

Bill Longley was either unimpressed by Hardin's reputation, eager for a little fun or doubtful that the man who had arrived in Evergreen that day was actually the famed outlaw. Upon seeing young Wes at the horse races, Longley swaggered right up to the notorious killer and, with his hand resting on the handle of his Dance revolver, spat out, "My name is Bill Longley and I believe you are a spy. If you don't watch yourself, you will be shot all to pieces before you know it!"

Hardin was known to kill for less than this, but sizing up the glowering man before him led him to do something that did not come naturally—he thought twice.

"You believe a —— lie and all I ask is that those who are going do the shooting get in front of me. And if your name is Bill Longley, I want you to understand that you can't scare me."

Everyone around the pair went silent; the air was heavy with the expectation of violence. The two men stood not two feet from one another. Their jackets were swept behind their holsters; their eyes were locked. But despite the suspense, the showdown between two of the deadliest men in Texas ended on an unexpected note.

Bill Longley smiled. "I see I have made a mistake. Are you here to see the races?"

Both men managed to keep their guns in their holsters, but their reluctance to draw on each other did not indicate any kind of lasting goodwill. On the contrary, tempers flared up again later that night when Wes beat Longley cleanly in a hand of poker and stripped him of $300. Harsh words were exchanged, but again neither man pulled his gun. Why did these men, who often looked for any excuse to kill a man, hold their guns when facing each other?

Who knows what mysterious forces motivated Longley and Hardin to do any of the things that they did. Hardin is reputed to have killed a man for snoring too loudly, and Longley once shot down a soldier for making a disparaging comment about Texas—yet neither man went for his guns in Evergreen that night, despite the open challenges. Perhaps Longley's observation of life on the frontier best explains the unspoken understanding that passed between

the two. In place of the law, a certain code of behavior emerged in the West that defined the way men related to each other. When writing of his experiences as a saloon-keeper in the mining town of Camp Brown, Wyoming, Longley wrote: "There was no law at all. It was simply the rule of claw and tooth and fang and the weakest went to the wall."

Both Longley and Hardin understood this code; as they stood face to face in Evergreen, perhaps they sensed that neither would prevail if it came down to gunplay. So they kept their hands close to their pistols and tested each other, prodding for fear or weakness, but neither budged. With survival the only ambition, Longley and Hardin kept their guns holstered, relying on their reputations to keep them out of trouble that night. After the horse races the next day, John Hardin rode out of Evergreen, bearing a contempt for his pistol-twirling rival that lasted a lifetime.

Though they were similar in many respects, Longley and Hardin were fundamentally different men. While Hardin was a social man who enjoyed the fame his homicidal reputation brought him, Wild Bill Longley was a stubborn recluse. Longley spent most of his time in solitude and sometimes went weeks on end without seeing a soul, only to murder soon after he was among other people. Constantly on the run from the law in Texas, Kansas, the Indian Territory and the Wyoming Territory, Bill was a true sociopath—always on his guard and deeply suspicious of everyone he met.

Longley reaffirmed his paranoia when he drifted into Bandera County, Texas in November 1875. He had been riding hard since April, when he had killed a childhood friend named Wilson Anderson in Bastrop County. Longley had spent the last seven months on the dodge and festering in his self-imposed isolation; by the time he rode into the hills of western Texas, he had killed four more men. Quickly getting work under an assumed name as a hired hand on the

Wadkins Ranch, he drove fence posts and repaired stables for two weeks, and then met Lon Sawyer, alias Will Scrier. Sawyer was an ex-gunfighter who had put away his revolver after he had claimed his first victim. Maybe the last stretch of solitude, dyed in sanguinary gunplay, was too much even for Longley's conscience, or maybe he just took a liking to the older man; whatever the reason, the outlaw confided in him, revealing himself to be none other than the infamous Bill Longley.

It was not long before Bill noted a change in Sawyer's behavior, and his obsessive mistrust began to take hold. He kept a close eye on his friend, and his suspicions were soon confirmed. Upon finding a discarded letter near Sawyer's cabin, Bill discovered that Sawyer had been writing to the Lee County sheriff, offering to help turn Bill in for a share of the $1000 reward on his head. Did Bill despair at this discovery? Or was he smug in the confirmation of his lack of faith in the men around him?

Whatever the case, Longley promptly rode to the sheriff's office in Uvalde and offered to catch the same Lon Sawyer who had shot a man dead on the Frio River—but only if the sheriff would deputize him. Thus, with a silver badge pinned under his jacket, the ruthless murderer went out to arrest the man who had tried to betray him. With the help of another deputy, Longley cornered a surprised Lon Sawyer on the road out of his cabin.

A smirk played across Longley's face as he swept back his jacket, revealing the deputy's star on his vest. He drew his six-shooter and sneered, "Throw up your hands, old man—you're my prisoner."

Sawyer sat in the saddle, paralyzed with shock. Then, with speed that caught even Longley off guard, he jerked his pistol and fired off a shot. As a bullet whistled dangerously close to Longley's ear, Sawyer growled, "I will see you in hell before you take me," and set spurs to his horse.

The other deputy lost control of his spooked horse, but Longley himself went after Sawyer and the two men continued to fire on one another as their animals ran at top speed. They tore through a cedar brake and over a clearing before both men's horses were shot out from under them. By the time Sawyer toppled off his horse, he had four bullets in his back but was still alive. Firing from the cover of cedar brush, Lon almost succeeded in ending Longley's life with a last-resort shotgun blast at close range. Indeed, it took no less than a bullet in the head to take the fight out of Sawyer. Later, Longley would state that Sawyer was the toughest gunfighter he had ever met. Riding into Uvalde, Bill collected his reward money, resigned his commission and promptly left the county.

Once more alone in the backcountry, Longley headed northeast towards an unexpected fate: In Delta County, the cold-blooded killer would fall in love. Bill stopped at a small farmhouse, near the town of Ben Franklin, late in the afternoon of February 12, 1876. Going by the name of William Black, he accepted old man Jack's offer to spend the night. It was during dinner that Longley would meet the beautiful Louvenia Jack. Instantly smitten by Louvenia's charm, the murderous outlaw considered something that had never before crossed his mind: reformation. Later, while in prison waiting for the gallows, Bill would write: "Not a wink of sleep came to my eyes that night. I never felt such feelings on earth as now seemed to take possession of me. I lay and thought of all my past life, and never before did I realize my true condition."

Creeping out of the Jack farmhouse at first light, Longley stole into the stable and drove a nail into his horse's hoof. Thus, at the time he was scheduled to leave later that day, Bill "discovered" that his horse was lame and his stay was conveniently delayed. Longley used the extra time to establish himself in the area. He started sharecropping for a preacher named Roland Lay and took up residence in the reverend's home. Meanwhile, he began courting Louvenia, and the possibility of spending the rest of his days in peace as a humble farmer began to seem feasible. Longley hung up his six-shooters for the farmer's rough plow handles and diligently put his back into the cotton field.

But by this time, trouble was a stray dog that Longley had fed too often; it always came back to bark at his door. Another man was interested in Louvenia Jack. Before Bill's arrival, a local badman had been engaged to be married to her. Although Louvenia's parents did not particularly like the man, Longley's rival was well established in the community. To complicate matters, Louvenia's erstwhile fiancé was Parson Lay's cousin, and the preacher himself strongly supported the match. Not knowing whom they were dealing with, the local boys in league with Lay's family tried to intimidate Longley by sending him threatening messages, warning him to stay away from Miss Jack. In the past, Longley would have answered with his guns, but love had tempered his hard nature and he remained silent. But as the months passed, threats mounted and the tension in the Lay household, where Bill ate and slept, became unbearable.

Finally, Bill responded. One hot, muggy day found Longley a little inebriated and heading out to Cooper for supplies when he ran into one of the most vociferous agitators of Lay's family. Longley began cussing at the surprised young man, who only wanted to get home. Before Bill let the man go on his way, he issued his challenge, roaring, "Tell every brother and uncle and other relative you have that I'll take the whole bunch, single-handed, anywhere and at any time."

Of course, this did nothing to ease the situation, and Longley soon realized his mistake. The threats got worse and his equipment was vandalized. When Parson Lay got in on the threats, Longley knew it was time to go. Collecting the money he had earned sharecropping, he rode north into Lamar County, just 10 miles from the Jack home. Longley did not intend to give up his pursuit of young Louvenia, but he felt that his move would take some of the pressure off the situation. He was wrong.

Parson Lay's family had assumed that Bill was gone for good, so when he rode back into town to visit the Jack farmhouse, the community erupted in anger. Roland Lay himself took action, informing the authorities that Longley had threatened his life before the move to Lamar County. The law arrested Bill when he got back home the next day. Afraid that his true identity would be revealed if he remained in jail, Longley escaped after six days in prison. Slipping into the night, Bill made his way to the parson's home without delay. He did not fight the anger anymore. Whatever gentility he had acquired in the calming presence of Louvenia evaporated in the pressure cooker of Delta County. Once again, Bill Longley was intent on murder.

Arriving at Parson Lay's farm in the early dawn, Longley stepped into the cow pen, taking position between Roland and his shotgun. The preacher looked up from where he was milking.

Raising his own shotgun, Bill addressed the old parson. "It's the end of the line for you, reverend. If you have anything to say, you had best be at it."

One look at the void in Longley's eyes and Lay knew he was a dead man. "I hate to die as much as the next man," he whimpered, "but please just promise me that you will leave my wife and family in peace."

Longley did not promise any such thing. In an almost detached curiosity, he asked Lay why he and his kin had not left him alone–but before he got an answer, he opened up with two barrels of turkey shot and killed the old man instantly.

It was to be Longley's last murder. In 1877 he was finally captured on the Texas–Louisiana border. He was dragged back to Giddings and given the death sentence for murdering Wilson Anderson in 1875. Something–it may have been his feelings for Louvenia Jack, or perhaps it was the specter of certain death that now loomed before him—inspired Longley to repent during his last year of life. He converted to Catholicism and spent long hours drafting letters of instruction to young men, warning them not to start down the path he had walked. He wrote of the mercy of God and his own debt to mankind. Even so, it was evident that Longley was still a man who tried to balance violent contradictions. He also wrote about a conspiracy of lies against him, his bitterness at receiving such a heavy sentence compared to Hardin's 25 years and his proud status as Texas' greatest outlaw.

Indeed, on the night before he was to be hanged, the condemned outlaw made a chilling confession to his prison guard. He admitted that, despite his claims of repentance, he regretted the murder of only one of the 32 men he had sent to the grave. The victim had been a cowboy who had the misfortune of camping with Longley for an evening. Bill could not sleep because he felt the strange drifter was watching him. Not willing to fall asleep while the cowboy was awake, and unable to stay up any longer, Longley nonchalantly drew his revolver and killed the man. The next day, Bill learned that the youngster had been on the lam and had been watching Longley for the same reason that Bill had watched him—namely, suspicion.

The contradictions within the psychotic outlaw were never resolved, even as the hangman's hood was placed over his head. Was he a repentant sinner or a proud killer? It did not seem to matter to the crowd at Giddings either way.

As the trapdoor opened, the hangman's rope slipped and Longley's feet scraped the ground. Hoisted back up by the hangman, Longley died by strangulation without the privilege of a broken neck. As he twitched for agonizing seconds at the end of the rope, the last thing he heard was laughter.

DAVE MATHER

3

DAVE MATHER

Thieving murderer one day and dedicated deputy the next, Mather was a man whose actions were dictated by whim, opportunism and a confused sense of righteousness.

Mysterious Dave Mather took a joke no better than he received a sermon. He was therefore not in the best of moods one hot summer Sabbath in 1877 as he squirmed on a hard wooden pew, the sole object of the Reverend Johnson's ardent gaze. Mather was not at all sure what to do about this holy man who was staring at him longer than any man in any saloon would dare; the stifled laughs of Dodge City's gambling men coming from the back of the church only infuriated him more. Dave's left eye began to twitch uncontrollably.

The evangelist was sweating heavily as he approached Mather, his voice straining under the heavy passion of his sermon and his arms extended, one outstretched hand just inches away from Dave's forehead. All of Dodge's devout were at church that Sunday, staring in horrified fascination at the unfolding drama. The famed Reverend Johnson was about to convert one of the town's most devilish residents to the Righteous Path. As for Mather himself, he decided at that moment that he'd had enough of this little show, and his right hand fell to the handle of his revolver. This was all a practical joke that had gotten out of hand, and events were about to take a decidedly Western turn.

The famous Reverend Johnson had arrived in Dodge just a few days earlier. Johnson was a man of such profound faith that he announced he could save the soul of "the wickedest man in the wickedest city in the world"—just point out the sinner and Johnson would do the rest on Sunday. Bat Masterson, the county's future sheriff, saw this as a perfect opportunity for a little fun and pointed out the scowling figure hunched over a pint of whiskey in the Long Branch Saloon. "There's your man, reverend," he said with a sly smile.

Mather probably smelled a rat when Masterson made it sound like all the gold that had been dug out of the Comstock Lode was awaiting him in church that Sunday. "We're all gonna be there, Dave," Bat said, gesturing to a group of the town's sporting men that were crowded behind him. "Word is that the preacher has something to say about us sinners." Masterson smiled broadly before continuing, "It's probably best that we show a united front for His Holiness, wouldn't you say?"

Bat had a rather outsized personality; he was the type of man to whom people had difficulty saying no. So when Sunday rolled around, Dave found himself seated right where the grinning Masterson had suggested, up at the front of the congregation, as he silently cursed whichever Christian it was who decided the Lord should be worshipped so early in the morning. After enduring the first half of the service in a fit of yawns, sighs and snarls, the liquor-addled badman was busy counting the years since he was last in a church when the pastor's booming voice interrupted his muddled calculations. Had Mather just heard his own name?

Dave's head snapped up to look at the altar. Sure enough, the parson was staring down at him—and every other person in the building was staring at him, too. Mather was about to assume that Johnson had been talking about David, King of Israel, when he heard Bat Masterson's snicker break the silence; it was then that Dave knew he had been duped. Mather was not sure what he was supposed to feel as Johnson began lecturing him personally—extolling the abundant Glory of God and the divine privilege of eternal life—but Dave, tired and hung over, grew more irritated with every word that rumbled from the cleric's throat. At the point in the pastor's sermon where Mather was supposed to finally see the light, leap to his feet and declare the purity of his newborn soul, Dave was thinking murder.

In the next moment, Mather was standing on the pew with his revolver in hand, celebrating his recent "conversion" by shooting out the lamps of the building and yelling out numerous hallelujahs over the roar of his six-shooter. Panic erupted among the parishioners and they ran for the doors, while Reverend Johnson and his deacons made an undignified exit, headfirst, through the church's stained-glass windows. Bat and a handful of his friends were the only ones left in the darkened building, howling with laughter at one of the strangest men in their sporting fraternity.

That night, Mysterious Dave Mather was celebrated as a hero in the Long Branch Saloon. The morning's events were told, retold and told again, the details of the account growing ever more preposterous as the hours were drunk down. In all the revelry, Mather alone kept his mouth shut about the incident. Tight-lipped and gimlet-eyed as ever, Dave was doing his best to focus on a poker game when one of the revelers managed to break through his taciturn shell with a single question: "So, Dave, death can't mean anything to you anymore, seeing as how your soul's in the hands of the Almighty."

When Mather cleared his throat to respond, everybody around him went quiet—the mysterious drifter was going to impart some of his wisdom. Some of those present may have been expecting to hear inspiring words from Dave, rumored as he was to be a descendent of the famous New England theologian Cotton Mather.

Mather began, intent on making some kind of sense despite the impressive volume of whiskey he had consumed that night. His gravelly voice rumbled through the saloon. "I never been afraid no how. I'm willin' to answer for anything I've ever done, and nobody can say I ever cheated 'em in words or cards." Glaring around the suddenly hushed bar, Dave finished his short speech: "If anybody wants to say otherwise, I'll kill him right now."

After a few moments of uncertain silence, a cheer rose in the room and Mather was instantly the recipient of a renewed onslaught of drinks. Satisfied that he had spoken his mind, Mysterious Dave turned back to the poker table, ready for the next hand.

If it is true that reticence is an indispensable part of the inscrutable man's character, then Mysterious Dave Mather's own reluctance to share his thoughts with others did much to earn him his nickname. But while Dave's silence may have been more an indication of a lack of inner dialogue than an overabundance of it, he was nevertheless an enigmatic gunslinger. Thieving murderer one day and dedicated deputy the next, Mather was a man whose actions were dictated by whim, opportunism and a confused sense of righteousness.

Mather spent as much time serving the law as he did running from it, and he did not seem to be bothered one bit by the constant shifting of his allegiance. Because he was directly descended from Cotton Mather, the famed Puritan colonial who had lived from 1662 to 1728, Dave was no doubt painfully aware of the way his life completely betrayed the esteemed memory of his ancestry. Even so, Dave seemed to entertain the notion that he himself was a virtuous man despite his abhorrent behavior. This self-delusion probably explains why the Reverend Johnson's assumptions about Mather's character had thrown Dave into a fit of rage, even though he was said to have never once lost his cool in a gunfight.

The ever-reserved Dave Mather's erratic motivations were certainly odd enough to earn him an aura of mystery among the whisperers, storytellers and bald-faced liars of the time. Yet it was also the end of his tale, so atypical of the gory conclusions that consumed most gunfighters, that set Mather apart from the average western badman. The last years of Dave's life were every bit as mysterious as his origins had been, and while there have been more than a few theories about what happened to Mather after his disappearance in 1887, not one of them has been backed by any hard evidence.

We know that Dave Mather was born in Connecticut in 1845; beyond that, not a single reliable word has been written about his formative years. As far as the history books are concerned, Mather just materialized in Sharp County, Arkansas, in 1873, rustling cattle and terrorizing locals with a hard gang of like-minded toughs. Either there was nobody on hand to record his exploits or Dave did little to stand out from the bandits with whom he rode, because not much has been said of his tenure on the Ozark Plateau. Certainly there was nothing about Mather that would catch a person's eye. Mather stood about 5'9" with dark features and a drooping mustache, and there was little in his build or features to suggest anything extraordinary. While Mather made it a habit to keep whatever thoughts he had to himself, he still indulged in enough dissolute behavior to confirm that he was not so different from the rogues with whom he associated.

After leaving Arkansas for unknown reasons, Mather was soon pursuing the same occupation that had drawn so many of North America's drifters in the 1870s—buffalo hunting. While stalking the Staked Plains of Texas in 1874, Dave apparently found the thrill of the hunt much less rewarding than the recreation to be had in the rowdy buffalo camps that served as the riflemen's headquarters. The newly established Dodge was just such a settlement when he rode into it that year—a motley assortment of canvas-topped business establishments, nestled among small mountains of buffalo hides and peopled by some of the roughest men on the frontier. But Mather developed an almost instant appreciation for the raw society in the burgeoning community, and Dodge would be the closest thing to a home that the rootless drifter would ever have.

Because he never strayed far from Dodge over the next four years, Mather was present when the settlement made its transition from shoddy buffalo camp to chaotic cattle terminus—going from bad to worse. It was a change that suited Dave just fine. As Dodge grew ever more wild and dangerous, Mather gambled, glowered, drank and murdered his way to a reputation.

Dodge didn't exactly welcome Mather with open arms; he was very nearly killed during his first weeks in Dodge when he was knifed in the gut during a gambling quarrel in 1874. Not long after he recovered, Dave apparently became preoccupied with the idea of justice. He formed a vigilance committee that sought to punish horse rustlers, and he was soon heading up lynching parties to execute men for the same crimes that he had been committing in Arkansas about a year earlier. He also served on the police force when things got hectic during the summer months, lending his support to men like Wyatt Earp and Bat Masterson in their numerous confrontations with rowdy Texan cowboys. And then there was the incident with Reverend Johnson in 1877, when Mather earned the distinction of being the only man in Dodge to ever draw his sidearms on a parson. Indeed, Dave managed to become one of the more talked about gambling men to ever swagger down Front Street. Amid whispers of his ancestry, roguish background and complete fearlessness, the assumption grew that his characteristic silence concealed some sort of dark, mysterious secret.

In the late summer of 1878, Mather's thoughts turned to moneymaking, and he left Dodge with Wyatt Earp during one of the legendary lawman's short forays out of town. Earp may have been impressed by Dave's withdrawn attitude, a certain laconic nature being something the two men shared. Or maybe he was just desperate for a business partner. Whatever the case, Wyatt invited Mather along for what he thought would be a sure-fire plan to make some easy money. On September 3, the two men were chased out of Mobeetie, Texas, by the town's marshal for selling fake gold bricks to gullible cowhands at $100 a pop. While Wyatt rode back into Dodge to resume his duties as a lawman, Mather was suddenly hit by an urge to change the scenery and so wandered west into Las Vegas, New Mexico, where he promptly acquainted himself with the local gamblers and lawmen.

When Dave Mather arrived in Las Vegas, the town was infested with some of the worst men in the West. Not only were outlaws such as Doc Holliday and Tom Henry regularly frequenting the town's saloons, but most of the peace officers were wanted men in other counties. The justice of the peace, Hoodoo Brown, held court in a saloon and used the butt of his Winchester as a gavel. The murdering John Joshua Webb was town marshal, and Dave Rudabaugh, the famous stock rustler and train robber, sometimes called on the aid of a Texan madman named Tom Pickett to help with his duties as town constable. After Mather was tried and found not guilty of train robbery late in 1879, he too decided to take up law enforcement in Las Vegas.

Recalling the bullying tactics he had learned while policing the streets of Dodge with Bat and Wyatt in Dodge,

Mather actually distinguished himself as a competent lawman during the last months of 1879. But it was not until January 1880 that Mather found himself in his first stand-up gunfight.

Dave was walking the evening beat with Joe Carson, one of Vegas' senior lawmen, when a bartender from the Close & Patterson Saloon ran up to the two officers, breathlessly informing them that the Henry Gang was whooping it up over at his bar—and that they were all wearing their guns in plain sight. The four-man Henry Gang had been on a vicious bender since riding into town a few days earlier, enjoying the fruits of almost certainly ill-gotten gains. Carson had already confronted them once about wearing their six-shooters in his place of business, whereupon the badmen had dutifully, if resentfully, surrendered their arms to the establishment for the night.

For whatever reasons, the gang did not feel nearly as accommodating this time around. Minutes after the two lawmen stepped through the saloon's swinging doors and demanded that the Henry Gang give up their firearms, the bar turned into a roaring battlefield. What exactly was said before bullets started flying is not known, but it is likely that the Henry Gang drew first because Joe Carson was hit twice before he got off a single shot. In the next few seconds, the air was saturated with lead as men on both sides of the fracas emptied their revolvers at each other. When the smoke cleared, Carson was lying dead, riddled with eight bullets. Two of Henry's boys lay dying on the saloon floor, and Tom Henry himself was obviously badly wounded; he left a trail of gore through the back of the bar while escaping with the last surviving member of his gang. Mather stood miraculously unharmed, his jacket torn at the shoulder in the spot where a single bullet had grazed him.

If the *Las Vegas Optic* marveled at Mather's uncanny luck the next day, the newspapermen had not seen anything yet. Only three days later, Dave would take down a man in what was probably the most incredible feat of gunplay in his entire life.

It was about 11 PM on the evening of January 25, and Joe Castello was trying his best to control the two railroad graders under his charge. The trio had been toiling on the Raton Pass extension of the Atchison, Topeka & Santa Fe Railroad when they decided to come into town for a break from the grueling work. They were soon roaring drunk, and in their inebriated state, the two graders realized that they despised each other. Castello found himself constantly trying to break up their quarreling as the night wore on. The three men were just about to enter another saloon when the two graders started bickering again and Castello suddenly found himself irritated to the point of murder. Drawing on his two employees, the foreman threatened to put a bullet in the next man who said a word. Taking stock of their now-common enemy, the pair seemed to decide that they did not like their boss too much either, and they responded to his threat by slowly moving their hands down to their own revolvers. Who knows what direction things would have taken if Dave Mather had not shown up at that instant, breaking through the crowd that had grown around the three inebriated men. Surprisingly enough, he was actually quite courteous.

"Excuse me, boys, but you best put up those guns right now. We've had more than enough trouble of late."

It is anyone's guess what Castello was thinking, but his reasoning was no doubt corrupted by the muddle of drink and the adrenaline rush of holding a loaded gun. He spun on his heels and leveled his weapon at Mather. "I don't think this is any of your business, so just be on your way."

Dave took one cautious step forward before he was stopped by the click of the weapon's machinery as Castello cocked the hammer. "You take one more step," Castello hissed, "and I'll shoot you where you stand."

Given what was about to transpire, maybe a few things should be said in Castello's defense. For one, he was completely juiced, and it is common knowledge that too much liquor impedes a man's reflexes. Secondly, the unfortunate foreman had probably never pointed a loaded gun at anyone before, let alone fired one. It can never be known if he had any intention of shooting at Mather, but his gun was loaded, the hammer was cocked and he felt comfortable enough to be making threats. As for Mather, his jacket was hanging over his Peacemaker and his arms were hanging limply at his sides. Castello could scarcely have had more of an advantage.

And yet Castello was not given time to blink, much less to make use of his advantage. Before the railroad worker could process what was happening, Mather swept his jacket aside, drew his pistol, cocked and fired, sending a single bullet tearing through the hapless man's innards and leaving him writhing on the dirt in front of his two former employees. Castello was dead by the following morning.

Dave Mather had won two gunfights in the span of three days, emerging unscathed as four men were relegated to the dust. His reputation had become large enough that he probably could have hung up his gun belt on that day and still gone down as one of the deadliest men in the region. But it is doubtful that Dave gave much thought to his place in history; he just kept on living the only way he knew how–by the gun.

The last remnants of the Henry Gang were spotted less than two weeks later. On February 6, John Dorsey and Tom Henry himself were dragged into the saloon/courtroom of Judge Hoodoo Brown, where they were remanded to prison until a court date was set for the murder of Joe Carson. The fugitives would not live long enough to hear the guilty verdict. In the early hours of February 7, Dave Mather was once again at the head of a lynch mob. After breaking into the Las Vegas jailhouse, he directed the enraged crowd with terse orders as they dragged the wounded men out of their cells. The next morning, Henry and Dorsey were found strung up to a windmill just outside of town, their lifeless bodies riddled with bullets.

By March, Dave had grown tired of the bloody little town of Las Vegas and was frequently heard complaining that he was not getting paid enough for his dangerous duties. So he set spurs to his horse once more, intent on seeing more of the country. After a short return to Dodge, Mather spent the next few years drifting from one town to the next, landing in varying degrees of hot water wherever he went.

For example, Mather was arrested in San Antonio in early 1881 for possessing substantial sums of counterfeit dollars. After a brief stint in the cooler, Dave was off again, this time finding work as an assistant marshal in the border town of El Paso. Before long, arguments over wages got in the way of his ability to do the job and Mather was once more on the road. He eventually drifted into Dallas, and found work pimping prostitutes in a brothel run by a woman named Georgia Morgan. He stayed long enough to win the madam's trust, then skipped town with her most valuable jewelry hidden in the bottom of his saddlebags and headed for the saloons of Fort Worth with his newfound riches. But he did not count on his former mistress' resourcefulness; Georgia Morgan somehow tracked down Dave's new address and appeared at his door with a loaded revolver in her hand. Without so much as a greeting, the enraged woman began mercilessly pistol-whipping the bewildered gunfighter with the handle of her Colt .45, stopping only when the building's proprietors physically tore her off Mysterious Dave. She was fined $8.25 for disturbing the peace, while Mather was extradited to Dallas and thrown into the calaboose for theft. But for whatever reasons, Georgia decided not to go ahead with her charges and Dave was eventually released from prison.

Deciding that he'd had enough of the rambling life, Mather moved back to Dodge City in June 1883. It is difficult to say how serious Dave was about making Dodge his permanent home. Although he took on a series of considerable responsibilities soon after arriving, it was not long before Dave slipped back into his destructive ways and quickly made any prospect of a stable life in the borough an impossibility.

To be sure, Mather's reputation served him well when he first returned to Dodge. He was appointed as both assistant marshal and assistant sheriff almost immediately after he arrived, and he also bought an interest in the Opera House Saloon. If things got off to a strong start in 1883, Mather's affairs began to unravel early in the new year. After losing his bid for the town constabulary in February 1884, Mather also lost his job as assistant marshal when Bill Tilgham beat out his boss, Jack Bridges, for town marshal in the April elections. Amid these defeats, Dave found himself embroiled in a quarrel with Tilgham's assistant, Tom Nixon, soon after the town's administration changed.

Mather's Opera House Saloon was in direct competition with Nixon's own dance hall, and the animosities stemming from the pocketbook added fuel to the fire of jealousy–Tom Nixon was certain that Mather had eyes for his wife. Bill Tilgham noticed the bitterness between Nixon and Mather one day when he caught the two glaring at each other from opposite ends of a bar. Tilgham walked up to his deputy and asked, "What's wrong, Tom?"

"It's my wife," Nixon muttered. "That wretch had better stay away."

The marshal was surprised at the suggestion. "Come now, Tom–you don't know anything, do you?"

"Not yet," Nixon growled back. "But he's always hangin' around."

Before Bill could question Nixon further, the assistant marshal wheeled about and stormed out of the saloon, never once taking his eyes off of Mysterious Dave, who nonchalantly returned his gaze.

Whether the affair between Mather and Nixon's wife was imagined or not, Nixon decided to take action. On Friday, July 10, Nixon was peeking through the window of the Opera House Saloon and scowling at Mather as the assistant sheriff went about his business. When Dave finally spotted Tom at his window, he strode outside and demanded to know the exact nature of the man's problem. After calling out a few derisive remarks, Nixon descended the short flight of steps that Dave was standing atop. Nixon spun around when he got to the ground floor, and it was only then that Mather noticed his rival had a revolver in his hands. Tom fired a single shot, but the bullet went wide and crashed into the woodwork next to Mather's head, showering him with splinters and singeing his face with the powder flash.

Nixon initially believed that he had murdered his perceived rival. He was quoted by the *Dodge City Times* the next day as saying, "I have killed Mather and I have no regrets."

But word got out that Mysterious Dave was still alive, and when Sheriff Pat Sughrue and Marshal Bill Tilgham came to arrest Nixon on July 21, the assistant marshal learned the truth. As the two lawmen escorted Nixon to the Dodge courthouse, Tilgham admonished his assistant. "With a man like Dave Mather, you ought to shoot straight or not at all. So you best watch out, because now he's on the hunt for you."

That same night, Tom Nixon was shot dead.

According to all the accounts, there was not much drama to the killing. It was about 10 PM and Nixon–having been released for lack of evidence connected to the attempted murder of Dave Mather–was walking down the street, close to where the Opera House was located. Mather simply came up behind him and said, "Oh, Tom…"

Before the assistant marshal could even turn to face Mather, the assistant sheriff drew and shot a bullet through

Nixon's back. Looking down at the lawman as he twitched in agony on the ground, Mather stared impassively at his mortally wounded quarry before methodically pumping three more slugs into his body.

This time Tilgham and Sughrue came to arrest the sheriff's deputy. On January 25, 1885, Mather was acquitted on a plea of self-defense after a lengthy trial.

After winning his freedom, Dave Mather was joined by a brother, Josiah; like his older sibling, Josiah seemed to materialize on the historical records from nowhere. Unfortunately, Josiah was not a calming influence on Dave.

By May 10 of that year, Dave Mather had apparently taken up his rambling ways again. He and his brother were in Ashland, Kansas, gambling and drinking in the popular Junction Saloon. Entangled in a losing round of cards, Dave did not take his defeat well at all, especially because his opponent—cocky and pink-cheeked David Barnes—was close to half his age.

Mather threw his cards at Barnes after losing the third round of the game and moved to scoop up all the money on the table. While young Barnes probably knew that he had been gambling with the one and only Mysterious Dave Mather, he could not find it in himself to let all this money go. "Hey," the youth protested, "who just won that last round?"

Barnes was not alone in the saloon; his brother John stepped up to lend his support upon seeing the tough spot in which his foolhardy sibling had found himself. Staring Dave Mather full in the face, John kept his voice steady and said, "That man has some friends here, and he won't be robbed in such a manner."

Dave Mather was in no mood to talk. He barely managed to mumble, "What have you got to do with this?" before shoving the young man out of his way. John tried to respond by yanking his six-shooter, but found his hands firmly restrained by the sheriff, who was determined to prevent violence. Meanwhile, Dave Barnes went for his gun and actually got a shot off at Mather before the veteran gunslinger could react. The bullet went just wide of Mysterious Dave's head, grazing his skull and burning a hole through his cowboy hat. That was all the damage the Mather brothers allowed the Barnes boys. Both Josiah and Dave Mather opened fire on David Barnes, killing him where he stood.

Shocked and sickened by the sudden eruption of violence, Sheriff Sughrue arrested Dave and Josiah on the spot. After preliminary hearings, bail was set at $3000; by the end of June, the brothers were again at large. They were obligated to appear in court for their trial in December, but neither brother would show up, which meant that they forfeited the $3000 they had scraped together to pay for their freedom.

Historical biographies of Mysterious Dave's adventures fail to give much information about what he did with his life after the murder of David Barnes. Some accounts have Dave returning to Dodge for a short while, intent on resolving a grudge he bore, against Bill Tilgham, the town marshal. Legend has it that Tilgham sent Dave scurrying out of town a few weeks later. If this anecdote is true, nothing was ever written of it in any of Dodge's newspapers. It is known that shortly after he jumped bail, Dave won the appointment of marshal in New Kiowa, Kansas, and served the town well for a few months.

Then there is a gap of a couple of years before Dave Mather resurfaces in Long Pine, Nebraska. It was the summer of 1887, and after riding into town alone, Mysterious Dave walked into E.B. Smith's hardware store to buy a knife and some ammunition. He got to talking with James Kerr, the store's clerk, who ended up inviting the lone gunslinger to stay at a cabin he owned some 20 miles out of town. Mather agreed, and the last descriptions of Mysterious Dave come from Kerr, who periodically visited the reclusive Mather up at his cabin. Kerr paints a picture of a man who had learned to completely embrace the solitude of his own company. Living in tranquil seclusion, Mather was said to come into town only when he needed to work for a little money; otherwise, he steered clear of the settlement and never even ventured into the local saloons. About a year had passed, and Kerr was just starting to get used to Mather's presence, when the silent killer vanished, never to be heard from again.

One theory of Mather's latter days has him joining the North-West Mounted Police in Canada, but Ottawa has no record of a Dave Mather ever having served in the federal police force. Another story has Mather dying in 1916 on his own ranch in Alberta. But the provincial authorities have not been able to produce any documentation that proves a Dave Mather was living within their borders at that time.

And that is where the raconteurs run out of ideas about Mather's final destination. Forced to leave this loose end dangling, perhaps reader and writer alike should allow Dave Mather this one last mystery.

4

BAT MASTERSON

Bat was only 17 years old, but the look in his eyes transcended his worldly experience. The predator is ageless in the moment he is about to kill.

Thick tendrils of cigar smoke curled above a densely packed crowd in the Kansas City saloon. The click of cards, clink of glasses and buzz of conversation competed with a piano player who was pounding out a cowboy's waltz on an upright next to the mahogany bar. It was the evening of November 14, 1881, and as the respectable citizens of Kansas City settled into their beds, the restless and rootless were filing into what could have been any one of the great western city's dens of iniquity. Driven by habit or desire, the borough's nocturnal denizens were too busy drinking, gambling and cavorting to notice the two men sitting at a corner table in the gas-lit bar. One was a reporter for the *Kansas City Journal*, sitting with his back to the door, nervously scribbling in his pad of paper whenever the other man opened his mouth to speak. Across the table

BAT MASTERSON

from the reporter, inattentively fiddling with an untouched glass of whiskey while keeping a sharp eye on everything around him, was Bat Masterson.

"So, then, Mr. Masterson," the journalist began, "rumor has it that you've gunned down 26 men out on the frontier." The reporter looked for a reaction from the young gunfighter who sat before him, but Bat's face remained expressionless. "Do you have anything to say about such a gruesome tally, Mr. Masterson?"

Decked out in a tailored suit with a derby perched haughtily on his head and a gold-headed cane resting against his chair, Masterson looked more like a Wall Street stock trader than a Front Street killer. Only the two Peacemakers in the heavy gun belt peeking out from under his jacket gave evidence of his violent past. Bat looked at the journalist for an instant before breaking into a warm smile that belied the dark rumors of his past. "So 26 is what they're saying, is it? Why, that would almost make one man for every year of my life." His gentle blue eyes lit up with what could have been either mischief or amusement. After downing his glass of whiskey, Bat gave his rather ambiguous reply. "While I don't suppose I've shot quite that many men, you could say I've had my fair share of...difficulties."

The article appeared the next day in the *Kansas City Journal* under the title "Bat's Bullets," and true to the spirit of artistic reporting so common to newspapers of that time, Masterson's reserved remarks had been transformed into a tale of high drama. The story would be reprinted in numerous papers from coast to coast—and then exaggerated further by several dime-novel authors. By the time America's melodramatic writers were done with him, Bat had a reputation that stuck long after he had hung up his shooting irons to pursue a more civilized career.

Bat certainly qualified as one of the more genteel drifters to roam the Great Plains, but any man wandering the windblown prairies of the United States during the 1870s would have been forced to come to terms with the violent realities of the time, no matter how refined his inclinations. For Bat and his two even-tempered brothers, Ed and Jim, life on the plains was a precarious balancing act, setting their congenial dispositions against the brutal necessities of survival. While all three adventurous and energetic brothers would distinguish themselves as plainsmen and peace officers in the West, Bat was the only Masterson who would go down in history as one of the region's most accomplished men. Guided by strong inner convictions, unerring loyalty to his friends, respect for the law, steady nerves and deadly proficiency with a six-shooter, Bat worked his way up from unknown railroad laborer to one of Kansas' most eminent lawmen. But in spite of the incredible feats that have been attributed to Bat and his smoking Colts–crediting him with dispatching anywhere from 26 to 38 souls–hard evidence confirms only a single man who fell under the muzzle of Masterson's guns.

Perhaps Bat's Canadian roots accounted for his moderate temperament. William Bartholomew Masterson was born on November 26, 1853, in the County of Iberville, in what is now Quebec. Lured into the United States by rumors of fertile land west of the Missouri River, Thomas and Catherine Masterson moved their family soon after Bat was born, eventually settling on a farm in Sedgwick County, Kansas. Bat and his big brother Edward were too young to join the army when the Civil War broke out in 1861, so while the Masterson family continued to grow throughout the 1860s, Bat and Ed became inseparable and enjoyed an idyllic life of hunting and fishing when they were not toiling away on their parents' farm.

Inevitably, the brothers became more restless as they grew older. In the summer of 1872, the eldest Masterson boys left home to sample what the world had to offer. Their first experience away from the farm taught them an important lesson about trust. Ed and Bat were hired by a subcontractor named Raymond Ritter to grade a five-mile stretch of the Atchison, Topeka & Santa Fe Railroad as it expanded across western Kansas. It was grueling work, but while the $300 commission—to be shared between the two of them—was hardly exorbitant, there is something to be said about the satisfaction of a hard-earned dollar. Ritter, however, seemed to think that work was reward enough in itself. When the boys staggered back into Dodge after completing the back-breaking job, they discovered that Ritter had skipped town and taken their $300 commission with him.

Sunburned, exhausted and now dead broke, the two boys stood in bewildered disbelief at the train station in Dodge. Ed was the kind of person who liked to think the best of people, so he was especially hurt by Ritter's deception. He was set on going back home and confessed that he was feeling homesick. "You better come with me, Bat," Ed said to his younger sibling. "Leaving's better than starving and being cheated out here."

The resignation in his brother's voice woke something mean in Bat; he was suddenly aware that he could not walk away from this situation. "Hell no, Ed," he roared. "You can go back if you want, but I'm going to stay here and lay for Ritter. That dog owes us $300, and he's going to pay up or I'll put a slug in him."

After assuring his brother that he would be fine by himself, Bat got a job as a teamster and hunkered down in Dodge while Ed went back home. Bat had reasoned that Ritter would have to come through Dodge eventually because he had contracts farther up the line. He did not have to wait long. Not a month had passed when a friend who worked for the railroad informed Bat that Ritter was on a train that would be coming into Dodge the next day.

The sun was just rising the following morning when the train pulled up into the Dodge station. Bat was there waiting with a brand-new Colt .45 strapped to his hip and a serious bone to pick. Jumping onto the train before it had stopped, he strode through the cars until he found the man he was looking for sitting at a window seat, idly staring outside. Masterson smiled in spite of himself. "Hello there, Raymond. Remember me?"

With these words, Bat lunged over the person sitting in the aisle seat, dragged Ritter through the passenger car, and threw him off the train and onto the station platform. By the time the crooked contractor had struggled to his feet, Bat was standing before him with his gun out. He was no longer smiling.

At first, Ritter tried indignation. "What is the meaning of–"

Bat did not let him finish. "You know damn well what this is about. You owe me and my brother $300. And I promise that if you don't pay up right now, there'll be one less jackass walking this earth."

Ritter sized up the wiry youth who stood before him and tried another ploy. "This is robbery, you whelp!" he yelled. Turning to the crowd that had gathered around them, the con man pleaded for someone–anyone–to get the marshal. "I'm being robbed in broad daylight," he protested.

Masterson suddenly became tired of dealing with the vile cheat. He pressed the muzzle of his Peacemaker against Ritter's forehead and cocked the hammer. "Not even 50 marshals could help you now, old man. Pay up or say your final prayers."

Bat was only 17 years old, but the look in his eyes transcended his worldly experience. The predator is ageless in the moment he is about to kill. Without another word, Ritter's shaking hands went for the massive roll of bills he had in his pocket. He was carrying more than $3000.

Trembling violently, he handed the entire roll to Masterson. But Bat's gun hand did not budge an inch. With his revolver still pressed against Ritter's forehead, Masterson shook his head. "Count out $300, Ritter," he snarled. "You don't owe me all of that."

Only after the contractor had counted out the Mastersons' wages and handed them over did the young man lower his revolver. As soon as the money was in his hands, Bat's expression softened. Smiling at his former employer, Masterson thanked him for his wages, tipped his hat and nonchalantly walked away, leaving Ritter wobbling on two shaky legs, a red impression of the muzzle of Bat's six-shooter still stamped on his forehead.

The story of the confrontation at the railroad station quickly spread through Dodge, and young Bat Masterson was soon being spoken of as a man not to be trifled with. For his part, Bat had gained a sense of his own capabilities from the confrontation with Ritter. While he had become aware that the world was populated with men who would say and do all sorts of things to get what they wanted, the standoff at the station left Bat with a feeling that he could still impose a little of his own sense of fairness through the strength of his actions. Young Bat Masterson could not have had any way of knowing how far he would eventually go with this attitude.

While he no longer had a taste for railroad work, it did not take Bat long to find another vocation. He joined up with a group of buffalo hunters in Dodge and spent the rest of 1872 earning his stripes in the buffalo camps. Slogging through his days as a buffalo skinner for one of the local outfits, Bat performed the unenviable work without complaint. It was the buffalo skinners' job to follow the hunters at a safe distance, so as not to spook nearby buffalo with the lumbering wagons they drove. After the hunters had shot 30 or 40 buffalo, they waved the wagons over, whereupon the skinners would have to strip the hides off every bloody carcass that lay on the prairie. The skinners scarcely had time to take the hides back to camp and stake them out to dry before the hunters had stalked another herd, leaving another batch of dead buffalo to be skinned. At this time, buffalo herds numbered in the thousands—often stretching as far as the eye could see—so the work was pretty much constant. Every day of the week for months on end, Bat cut his way through the gory, grubby work.

For the most part, Bat did not have much to say to the men with whom he toiled on the plains. He did not mind drinking himself into a besotted stupor, but the inevitable cost of such revelry the next day prevented him from making it a habit. Bat was not the type of man who would brag about how many Indians he had killed, nor did he enjoy brawling for brawling's sake. What's more, he tried his best to keep himself clean. In short, Bat did not fit in too well with the rough characters who populated the buffalo camps. While his work ethic and reputation guaranteed him a certain degree of respect, Masterson became something of a loner during this period of his life. This is not to say that he did not make any friends, but Bat chose his friends carefully, forming alliances with men whom history would remember as the greatest of the drifters who rid the plains of the buffalo.

Billy Dixon was one of the few people Masterson would call a true friend during his tenure with the bison trade. Dixon was known as an expert marksman with the .50-caliber Sharps rifle that was the buffalo hunters' weapon of choice. A reserved man who kept his distance from the other hunters, Dixon had the same silent intensity about him when he was resting in the camps as he did when staring down the barrel of his rifle at a buffalo. Unlike so many of his associates, Dixon's ambitions reached further than the next glass of whiskey. While he never achieved the fame of men like Wyatt Earp or Wild Bill Hickok, Bat would later describe Dixon as a "frontiersman of the highest order." The greatest obstacle that stood between Bat and a similar distinction was his periodic struggle with homesickness.

It was during a particularly rough patch of such melancholy that Bat befriended Wyatt Earp. The laconic frontier veteran—who did not think much of anybody—saw something he liked in young Masterson. Perhaps Wyatt recognized a bit of himself in the greenhorn frontiersman. Though still a teenager, Bat carried himself with a gravity that belied his years; his eyes shone with a sensitive thoughtfulness, and while he was not given to preaching, it was obvious he held firm convictions that governed his daily behavior. If Bat lacked the ferocious demeanor for which Wyatt was so famous, he was in command of formidable mental and physical strength. No man crossed Bat lightly. Wyatt's confidence in Bat's character was not misplaced; Masterson would come to be one of Earp's most loyal friends, standing side by side with the famous lawman against hell-raising cowboys during Dodge City's wildest years.

But for the time being, Bat was just a homesick teenager making do the best he could. Not that he was doing that badly—by the following year, Bat had grown confident enough with his knowledge of the hunt to set up his own outfit with his big brother Ed and his younger brother Jim. Bat and Ed did most of the hunting, while the unpleasant task of skinning fell to the youngest brother, who had just turned 18 years old. Because they had all been raised with the same values and blessed with the same easygoing nature, the brothers had no difficulties working together. From these humble origins on the plains, all three Mastersons would eventually rise to prominence among the drifters in the West.

Bat was the first brother to become a celebrity in Kansas. He had not been back home since he had left with Ed in the summer of 1872, and it seemed that he was definitely getting over his youthful homesickness. While Ed and

Jim started back for the family farm after a lean Christmas Day celebration on the prairie, Bat rode to Dodge, hoping to take up with another hunting outfit. He ran into Billy Dixon on Front Street soon after he had arrived, and it was not long before Bat had a place as a hunter on Dixon's team.

But it was now 1874, and the massive buffalo herds that had dominated the landscape in 1870 were already whittled down considerably. Dixon's crew went as far south as the Texas Panhandle to get at buffalo that had sprawled all over western Kansas just four years prior. Operating out of the famous buffalo camp of Adobe Walls, about 150 miles southwest of Dodge, Dixon and Masterson did not make a single kill until May of that year. Word quickly spread that a herd had been spotted, and soon all the hunters in the Walls were out for the slaughter. As they began shooting their lumbering quarry, the hunters were unaware that three pairs of eyes were watching them coldly.

Quanah Parker was one of the most respected Indian chiefs on the southwestern plains. The half-white Comanche leader had long borne an especially virulent hatred for aggressive American expansion. That summer morning as he watched the white men joyfully wiping out the dwindling sustenance of his people, it was obvious to Parker that the government had failed to keep its promise to rid the buffalo hunters from his territory. Staring with disdain at the wasteful spectacle before him, Quanah Parker signaled the two war captains that were with him. The three Indians turned their mounts away, their faces reflecting thoughts of vengeance.

In the following weeks, the hunters at Adobe Walls began to grow anxious. There were ever-increasing sightings of large Indian bands riding through the Panhandle, and men brought word of scalped hunters found rotting next to buffalo carcasses. The hunters hunkered into the Walls, choosing not to break for Dodge because they did not want to miss what they knew would be one of the last buffalo hunting seasons in America, but their forays for buffalo were becoming shorter and less lucrative as the fear of roaming Indians increased. Bat was in James Hanrahan's saloon when an army sergeant and four bluecoats rode in to confirm the hunters' worst fears—Quanah Parker had united braves from the Comanche and Southern Cheyenne and was on the warpath. It was likely that he would ride on the Adobe Walls.

The men took the dark news in silence. The first thing that occurred to anyone was that Nancy Olds, the only woman in the camp, had best head back to Fort Supply with the soldiers. Not only was she suffering from a horrible toothache but, if the attack should come, the hunters deemed that the ensuing bloodshed would be no sight for a woman's eyes. Nancy, who was the cook in the restaurant owned by her husband, William Olds, and an experienced frontierswoman in her own right, would hear nothing of leaving the Walls. "I came out here with Mr. Olds to make a living, and come cowboys, Indians or Lucifer himself, we intend to stay out here." William Olds stood beaming with pride at his wife. "If the tooth gets worse," Nancy continued, "I'll have one of you men pull it out with a pair of pliers."

So the party of 39 in Adobe Walls remained intact when the soldiers left the next morning. The Walls itself was no more than a handful of windowless sod houses built in an abandoned trading post, surrounded by weathered walls that stood about five feet tall. The main buildings in the settlement were a saloon, a restaurant, a trading post and a smithy. In the late spring of 1874, everyone in the camp slept closely around the buildings and regular watches were posted at the walls. Though it was not much as far as forts went, this tiny camp in the middle of hostile territory was the only haven the hunters had, and no one dared stray too far.

Nothing happened throughout May and much of June. Growing tired of gambling, horse racing and sharpshooting contests, the men eventually settled into Hanrahan's and started working their way through his stores of homebrewed whiskey. As supplies of the saloon's vicious rotgut began to run low—and as it became increasingly clear that the buffalo had moved on to the north—the trapped hunters grew edgy. There were tense moments over such trifling matters as whose turn it was to buy the next round, who had shot more buffalo in his lifetime or who could consume the most booze. Furthermore, the men had been gambling the entire time they had been cooped up, so grudges naturally accumulated with poker debts. If the Indians had not come when they did, the hunters might well have done Parker's work for him.

June 26, 1874, was a warm summer's night. The Walls' residents were fast asleep, their blankets crowded around the camp's four establishments. Most of the men were in deep, alcohol-induced slumber, sending a multitude of heavy snores drifting over the plains, when a loud cracking report woke everyone in an instant. Dixon and Bat were up in a flash, frantically searching the dark with their guns drawn and ready. But instead of Indians, burly old James Hanrahan came lumbering out of the darkness. Informing the men that a ridgepole supporting the roof in his saloon had just cracked, Hanrahan warned them that if they did not repair it quickly, all the remaining whiskey in camp would soon be buried under the remains of his establishment.

The sun had just begun to peek over the eastern horizon when the hung-over frontiersmen finished their task. Cursing the light, the hunters had just begun heading back to their crude beds when Dixon shouted a warning and lunged for his Sharps rifle.

Every one of the men looked to the east, where more than 200 horsemen galloped towards them with the rising sun at their backs. At last, the Indians were coming.

In moments of barely restrained panic, the hunters grabbed their rifles, dashed into the nearest buildings and began piling bags of flour and grain against the doors. By the time the best shooters were at the portholes of the sod houses, the war whoops and thundering hooves of the war party were all around them.

If there is any truth to the number of dead men who have been attributed to Bat's guns, the vast majority of those men fell on this day. Masterson was positioned at the same window as Dixon in Hanrahan's Saloon and, with a calm, unflinching eye, opened up on the first clear target he had. He would continue firing for more than three hours. While a running horse is a trickier target than a grazing buffalo, most of the men in the four buildings were proficient riflemen; as the braves tried crashing their horses through the front doors, shooting through the buildings' windows or barreling against the sod walls themselves, the withering fire from the houses began to take a toll on Parker's band.

Three hours later, the Indians finally ceased their attack on the frazzled gunmen, leaving more than 30 dead warriors strewn around the Walls as they retreated. The hunters had been hung over and trapped in smoke-filled houses, but they had lost only four of their number: Two teamsters who had been camped outside the walls were killed soon after the Indians began their attack; a young man named Billy Tyler had taken an Indian bullet in the chest; and Nancy's husband, William Olds, had shot himself accidentally while loading his rifle.

Bat's career on the plains would quite likely have been cut short if Hanrahan's ridgepole had not cracked, waking everyone in the camp just before Parker's braves swooped down upon them. Luck was with the hunters at Adobe Walls that morning, however, and most of them lived through the opening battle of the Red River uprising, a bloody campaign for mastery of the southwest plains that lasted throughout the rest of 1874 and 1875.

Many of the hunters who fought at Adobe Walls felt they had seen enough frontier adventure to last a lifetime, and those who had homes headed back to them in search of tamer pursuits. Bat Masterson, on the other hand, was just getting started. He and Billy Dixon enlisted as scouts in General Nelson A. Miles' Indian Territory Expedition, and Bat spent the next year reporting Indian movements, carrying dispatches and guiding soldiers to outposts. Masterson managed to keep himself alive through the campaign, but the tough experience killed the boy in him. Hardened by near-constant death and danger, Bat traded his innocence for the tough-minded simplicity of the frontiersman.

The Indian trouble was resolved when the Comanche and Cheyenne were forced back into their reservations during the harsh winter of 1875. Bat spent the rest of the year scraping out a meager living from the quickly disappearing buffalo before deciding to settle down in the rough town of Sweetwater, Texas, for the following winter.

Sweetwater owed its existence to the patronage of two groups—buffalo hunters and the soldiers from nearby Fort Elliot. The borough's sole purpose was to provide entertainment for these feral men, a business that was aided by the fact that there was no lawman or municipal government to be found in the coarse town. It was an ideal site for Masterson's first and only real murder in a six-gun shoot-out.

It was early January 1876 and Bat was in the Lady Gay, one of the more popular dance hall/saloons in town, when he first noticed Molly Brennan. A striking young woman with dark hair and blue eyes, she would have received a lot more attention from the men around her if it were not for her relationship with Melvin A. King. Corporal King was a cavalryman stationed in Fort Elliot, a gunfighting soldier who prided himself equally as a veteran of the Civil

War, a survivor of a number of Indian campaigns and the perpetrator of more than one liquor-fueled shooting scrape. Vociferous, violent and short-tempered, the corporal was rumored to have killed several men in saloon disagreements. When Bat rode into town, King was one of the most respected regulars in Fort Elliot–and one of the most feared gunfighters in Sweetwater. Young Molly Brennan initially found herself drawn to the brutish corporal and the nervous respect he got from other men, but she soon tired of King after coming to know the depraved character behind the bravado. Whatever affection Brennan may have had for the corporal vanished the moment she saw Bat Masterson smiling at her from across the gambling room in the Lady Gay.

For his part, Bat was not at all deterred by King's reputation, and within weeks the boorish corporal found himself nursing his wounded pride and a broken heart as Molly forgot about him completely. The whispers and sidelong smirks aimed at him in Sweetwater did not sit well at all with King. He added generous dollops of whiskey to the bitter stew of jealousy, and the end of January saw the corporal on an ugly bender that had imminent bloodshed written all over it.

On the evening of January 24, 1876, Bat and Molly were the last customers in one of the town's saloons, enjoying a quiet moment over a few glasses of whiskey while the bartender was closing up. Their conversation was interrupted when they heard a series of forceful knocks at the door. Uttering a few derisive remarks about the dedication of drunks to their craft, Bat made his way to the bar's entrance. Molly may have had a bad premonition when she heard the muffled yell outside, but if she recognized the voice, she was not quick enough to stop Bat. Masterson opened up the door to inform whoever was on the other side that the saloon was closed, but he soon found himself backpedaling as Melvin King stumbled into the bar–red-eyed and reeking of booze–with an ugly leer on his face and a cocked Colt .45 in his hand.

King was cursing everything in creation in an incoherent litany of rage as he staggered into the saloon, but if Melvin's whiskey-addled speech was unintelligible, his murderous intent was all too clear. He tried to give Bat another earful, but all that came out was a loose thread of stammered syllables and a generous dose of drool. In light of how drunk the cavalryman was, Bat may well have been able to handle the situation, but Molly panicked. Jumping in front of Masterson, she cried out to her former beau, "Don't shoot, Mel, you're drunk!"

Molly's sudden movement reminded King why he was there in the first place, and he responded by firing his pistol at her. A single slug tore through the woman's stomach and lodged itself in Bat's pelvis, shattering his pelvic bone. The crazed soldier was able to fire only once–even before Molly hit the ground, Masterson peeled his Peacemaker from its holster and blasted a hole into King's chest, killing him instantly. Seconds later, all three players in the love triangle were crumpled on the blood-soaked saloon floor.

The bartender was the first to see the grisly aftermath of the battle–one man dead, one woman dying and Bat Masterson sitting against the sod wall with his hand pressed against his wound. "I think he killed her," was all Bat was able to say before he passed out. While Molly Brennan did indeed die of her wound, Bat was released from Fort Elliot's hospital in the spring of 1876.

It is difficult to gauge the impact Molly Brennan and Melvin King had on Masterson. After the debacle at Sweetwater, he did develop a pronounced animosity for loudmouthed toughs; it is also true that he did not marry until he was 38, which was fairly old for a man in those days. But if Bat was going through any kind of profound grief, he did not talk about it. The only visible scar he took with him from Sweetwater was a limp from the bullet that had shattered his pelvic bone.

Not long after he was discharged from the hospital, Bat wandered north from the Texas Panhandle and changed his career from buffalo hunter to peace officer. The number of inebriated cowpunchers had begun to outnumber the heads of bison on the plains, creating a need for brave men who knew their way around a six-gun. Bat got work as Wyatt Earp's deputy in Dodge City later that year, and he limped through the town's streets with an oak cane in his left hand and a no-nonsense look in his eye. Exchanging the rough buckskin garb of the buffalo hunter for the tailored fashions of an urbanite, Bat fit easily into his new life in law enforcement. So it was that the next nine years of Masterson's life moved in a loose orbit around the one town in the West that was most in need of a good law officer.

Bat served his first tenure as a lawman in the summer of 1876 under the tutelage of Wyatt Earp. Masterson's approach to lawbreakers was greatly influenced by his hardheaded mentor, and Bat would not kill a single man in all the years he served as a peace officer. While Earp was renowned for the practice of "buffaloing" his inebriated quarry with the barrel of his revolver, Masterson used his cane to the same effect. Indeed, many of Masterson's chroniclers attribute his nickname to his habit of using the cane as a law-enforcement tool on the heads of unruly Texans, but his brothers had shortened Bartholomew to Bat long before he pinned on a silver star in Dodge. By the time the summer of 1876 was over, Bat's natural intolerance for extreme debauchery had been hardened by the numerous confrontations with Texans he'd had through the season. His experiences in Dodge left Bat as fearless, unflinching and uncompromising as Wyatt Earp himself.

Bat left Dodge during the slow winter months to try his luck at the gold rush in the Black Hills, and a lot had changed in town by the time he rode back into Kansas for the next cattle season. For one thing, both Jim and Ed were now residents of Dodge City, having been lured by the adventure and opportunity the thriving cattle terminus seemed to offer. Jim had capital invested in a saloon/dance hall, while Ed had been appointed as a deputy marshal. Wyatt split the summer between prospecting for gold in the Black Hills and manhunting an outlaw named Dave Rudabaugh; consequently, Bat's best friend was absent from the cattle town for long stretches that season. Meanwhile, Charlie Bassett had announced that he would not seek reelection as Ford County's sheriff in November, thereby leaving the office up for any takers.

  Bat ran into Wyatt riding up into the Black Hills with his brother Morgan, and the trio spent a quiet night camped out on the plains of Nebraska. When Masterson told Wyatt that he was going back to Dodge for the summer, the laconic lawman suggested that Bat should run for sheriff of the county. Bat looked surprised. "But I'm not even 23," he protested.

  Wyatt sized up his tough apprentice for a moment before responding, "You're as much a man as you'll ever be."

  If the exchange left any impression on Masterson, he did not start his campaign season auspiciously. In fact, he had barely arrived in town when he made an enemy of Larry Deger, Dodge's corpulent town marshal.

  It was June 6, and Bat had been celebrating his return to Dodge with a tour of the town's saloons. He was just stumbling out of the Long Branch when he ran into Bobby Gill, a diminutive Dodge resident who was famous for his sense of humor. Cranked up on booze, Gill was giving an impromptu stand-up act dwelling on the prodigious poundage of their town's obese marshal. Gill had the crowd around him howling, but the comedy did not sit well with Marshal Deger, who just happened to be lumbering by at that very moment. Using more than a little excessive force,

Deger arrested Gill on dubious charges and started out for the town jail. Upset that the show was over—and disturbed about the flimsy allegations Deger was slapping on Gill—Bat decided to get involved.

Bat broke through the crowd of spectators and locked his arm around Deger's neck, allowing Gill to make an escape. Deger managed to get Bat off of him pretty quickly and, with the help of a few bystanders, gave Masterson an ugly beating before dragging him to the calaboose. That same day, Ed Masterson, acting as Deger's deputy, caught up with Bobby Gill and threw him into a cell with Bat, who was doing his best not to take his brother's actions personally.

Little did Bat know that his fight with Larry Deger had put him in high esteem with some of Dodge's most powerful men. James Kelley, the town mayor and owner of several local saloons, was not overly fond of the overbearing marshal or the way he went about his duties. Because Deger was also a saloon owner, the rotund marshal represented an opposing business interest in town. Worse, Deger was not above using his station to promote his own saloon at the expense of his competitors. He once went so far as to arrest the bartender in one of Mayor Kelley's saloons on trumped-up charges so that he could get customers into his own establishment, where the bartender was conveniently not in the jailhouse. When Kelley found out that the young man who had stood up to Deger was the same Bat Masterson who had taken his wages at gunpoint from Raymond Ritter years earlier, fought at the battle of Adobe Walls and killed the notorious Melvin King, the mayor took the popular frontiersman under his wing.

With the endorsement of Dodge's mayor and the influential business interests he represented, Bat was appointed undersheriff of Ford County and declared his intention to run for sheriff in the fall election. The *Dodge City*

Times lent Masterson strong support: "Bat is well known as a young man of nerve and coolness in cases of danger. He is qualified to fill the office and if elected will never shrink from danger." Masterson seems to have been less adroit at the art of politicking. "I have no pledges to make," he wrote in the *Times*, "as pledges before an election are usually considered to be mere claptrap."

Fortunately, Dodge was not looking for a master rhetorician, and on November 6, 1877, Masterson beat out Larry Deger for the sheriff's office, winning by only three votes. His first act as sheriff was to fire Dodge's marshal and appoint his big brother Ed Masterson to the position. Thus the two eldest Masterson brothers went from low-ranking policemen in the spring to two of the most powerful lawmen in the county by fall. But with these accomplishments came more responsibility and more risk—in a time and place when simply looking at a man the wrong way could be risky enough. Though none of the brothers knew it, a dark shadow had passed over the entire Masterson family the day Bat won the county seat.

It would be a hectic year for the law in Ford County. While Bat boosted his reputation with the capture of four train robbers shortly after his inauguration, Ed found himself struggling to keep the lid on Dodge. Bat and Ed were similar enough; both were tough, frontier-bred men imbued with steady nerves and remarkable courage. But where Bat had a healthy respect for the evil of which men were capable, Ed was cursed with a tendency to assume the best about people. When Bat was confronted with an ornery Texan, he would usually knock the man down before too much was said. Plenty of Texans developed a resentment for this swift, uncompromising procedure, but at least Bat could boast that he never had to shoot a cowboy. Ed, on the other hand, was of such a genial disposition that he believed he could talk most offenders into seeing the foolishness of their actions, allowing him to peacefully walk, instead of drag, his quarry to the calaboose. Ironically, Ed's kindlier approach to the work of law enforcement resulted in more bloodshed than Bat's tough tactics.

In November 1877, Ed was in the Lone Star Dance Hall, trying to convince a man named Bob Shaw to quit shooting at a gambler called Texas Dick. Even though Shaw was standing by the entrance and Ed could have cut the fight short by rushing in and buffaloing him, the eldest Masterson preferred the gentler art of persuasion. Unfortunately, Shaw was both roaring drunk and convinced that Dick had cheated him of $40. Words were getting nowhere; after a short verbal exchange, Bob ended up turning his revolver on Ed. Masterson got a bullet through the right arm for his kindness, and he had to shoot Shaw through the arm and leg to resolve the issue.

Of course, Bat was exasperated with his elder sibling after he heard the news of the fight. What Ed called "the quality of mercy," Bat dubbed plain stupidity. He tried to sell the merits of swift violence to his brother: "Let this be a lesson to you, Ed. If you would've cracked that swine's skull instead of wasting your breath on him, there wouldn't have been a single shot fired."

"Bat," Ed said with his broad Masterson grin, "you sound exactly like Wyatt."

Bat was not amused. "Damn it, Ed, you listen to me. I worry about you!"

Much to Bat's sorrow, his concern would eventually be justified. Five months later, Bat found himself pushing his way through a crowd milling around Hoover's Saloon so that he could be with Ed during his brother's last moments of life.

Earlier that night, Ed had peacefully disarmed a cowboy named Jack Wagner. After giving the revolver to Alf Walker, Wagner's trail boss, he explained the city ordinance about checking firearms past the Dead Line. Not an hour later, Ed spotted the same cowpunchers on Front Street and noticed that Wagner was carrying his shooting iron once again. This time, the exchange was not a peaceful one; rather than hand over his revolver, Wagner pressed the muzzle against Ed's abdomen and fired, sending a bullet into the right side of his stomach and out the left. While Masterson was reeling back, his jacket on fire from the muzzle blast, he drew and got four shots off, cutting Wagner down with a shot through the gut and riddling Walker with three slugs from his .45. Both men crumpled and would eventually die of their wounds; Ed, his jacket still aflame, staggered 200 yards to Hoover's Saloon, where he finally collapsed. He was dead an hour later.

The Mastersons did not let Ed's death deter them from their duties in Dodge. Later that spring, Jim joined the police force; he would eventually take over Ed's old job as town marshal. As for Bat, he was not given much of a chance to mourn his brother's death because his own responsibilities as sheriff kept him too busy to dwell on the frailty of human life. Given Bat's line of work, this lack of reflection was probably a good thing—he was often forced to face the possibility of his own death at the hands of any depraved desperado who thought he was bigger than the law.

Early in 1879, Bat's job could have very well cost him his life when he confronted the notorious Ben Thompson during one of the Texan's infamous drinking binges. Thompson had flipped his lid in Ben Springer's Comique Hall when a performer named Eddie Foy started making cracks at his expense. Spitting obscenities, Thompson drew his weapon and would have certainly killed the comedian if Bat had not been there to grab Ben's pistol by the muzzle and yank it out of his hand. Thompson could only stare in disbelief as the stoic sheriff smiled at him. "Let me invite you for a walk outside, Ben," Bat said. "It's a nice cool night."

Though Thompson's other Colt was still in its holster, there was something about Masterson's utter lack of fear that made him think twice about gunplay that night. "You know, sheriff," Thompson slurred, "I think that's a fine idea." Somehow, the two men would become fast friends.

While Thompson was able to overlook the fact that Bat was a lawman and a Yankee, another famous Texan gunslinger was never able to appreciate Masterson's personality. Late in the summer of 1878, the homicidal Clay Allison, also known as the "Wolf of the Washita," rode into town to avenge the death of George Hoyt, a cowboy whom either Jim or Wyatt had cut down in a confused gunfight some weeks earlier. Probably because Bat was the highest police authority in Dodge, Allison became fixated on the idea of putting him alone on Boot Hill as an example to those who thought of messing with his Texan brethren. Wyatt was itching to go up against the legendary Allison on his own, but Bat's levelheaded temperament won the day. He wanted no blood spilled in retaliation for the death of Hoyt.

As Clay sauntered down Front Street for his much-anticipated meeting with the county sheriff, he could not help but notice the small army of lawmen that had gathered with all sorts of loaded weapons along the storefronts of Dodge's main drag. The town was suddenly quiet as Bat stepped out of the Long Branch Saloon and began to walk down the middle of Front Street with a hard look in his pale blue eyes. By this time, Clay was becoming painfully aware of the hopelessness of his situation.

Bat called out a greeting: "Here I am, Allison. Now what was it you wanted to say to me?"

The Texan gunfighter remained silent and just kept on walking towards Bat, trying his best to look nonchalant. Allison then walked right up to—and right past—Masterson, tipping his hat to the sheriff as he strutted by and moseyed straight out of town. Wyatt Earp broke the silence with a loud snort, and then the whole town let out a collective sigh of relief. Bat was standing out on the street with a wide smile on his face, trying his hardest not to break into laughter. So went the Wolf of the Washita.

It seems that Bat's exceptional talent as a lawman was matched with an especially difficult tenure as sheriff. When he was not chasing down train robbers, horse rustlers and murderers, Bat was breaking up brawls in Dodge City, pursuing Cheyenne across the plains as a deputy federal marshal or putting his guns behind the Santa Fe Railroad when the company clashed with the Denver & Rio Grande. He even found time to do Ben Thompson a personal favor by springing Thompson's rabid little brother, Billy, from the jailhouse in Ogallala, Nebraska, after the younger Thompson had killed a man in a homicidal fit.

But despite Bat's dedication to his job, the citizens of Ford County did not elect him for a second term. Beset by allegations of fraud, wasteful spending and use of excessive force against citizens, Masterson lost his position to George Hinkel. Hinkel was a sluggish saloonkeeper whose only real credential was the support he got from Dodge City's reform faction, which aimed to break up James Kelley's grip on the town. The election was an ugly one, with the reformers' paper, the *Spearville News*, hurling all kinds of invective at Masterson, who tried to maintain a dignified silence. Voters seemed to take Bat's reticence as an admission of guilt, and Hinkel won the election by a wide margin.

While Bat may have carried himself admirably throughout his term, it cannot be said that he exited his office with a great deal of grace. Writing a letter to the *Dodge City Times*, Masterson vented his anger at Bob Frey, one of the reformers' principal mudslingers and editor of the *Spearville News*:

In answer to the publication made by Bob Frey of the *Spearville News* asserting that I made threats that I would lick any s– of a b– that voted or worked against me the last election, I say it is as false and flagrant a lie that was ever uttered; but I did say this: that I would lick him, the s– of a b–, if he made any more dirty talks about me; and the words, s– of a b–, I strictly confined to the Spearville editor, for I don't know any other in Ford County.

Frey was said to have responded to the insult by going out and buying a newfangled self-cocking revolver, boasting to a number of people that he intended to use it on Bat the next time he saw him. When Masterson got wind of the newspaperman's bravado, he merely laughed. "Tell Bob he best wait 'til they make a self-loading cannon before he decides to take anyone on."

Though Masterson drifted out of Kansas after the 1879 election, he had put too much of his heart into Dodge to ever leave the borough behind completely. As long as he was in the West, Bat felt the memories of Front Street tugging at the wilder part of his consciousness, and he would return on more than one occasion to set matters as he saw them straight.

Bat rode up to Leadville, Colorado, during the winter of 1880 and stayed to make his living at the card tables in the mining camp's saloons during its legendary boom years. Many of the town's more than 40,000 miners were making millions from the enormous silver deposits in the surrounding mountains. After a move from the snowy crags around Leadville to the dusty hills in Cochise County, Bat spent the next year down in Tombstone, Arizona, dealing faro in Wyatt Earp's Oriental Saloon. He probably would have been one of the gunmen at the OK Corral if not for an especially provocative telegram he got from Dodge early in 1881.

Jim Masterson was having personal problems with the two men with whom he owned a dance hall. An anonymous friend got word that Jim's business associates, A.J. Peacock and Al Updegraffe, were planning to take care of Jim permanently and wired Bat to warn him that his brother's murder was imminent. Bat was on the next train out of Tombstone and he arrived in Dodge on April 16, at 11:50 in the morning. Spying the two would-be assassins almost the moment he got off the train, Bat did not bother with any small talk. Hauling his Peacemakers from their holsters, Masterson roared across the station, "I've come over a thousand miles to settle this, so you dogs had best get to defending yourselves."

The pair barely had time to pull their own revolvers before Bat unleashed a one-man fusillade. The ensuing gunfight was brought to a quick conclusion after Updegraffe took a bullet in the lung and Peacock turned tail and ran. Bat left Dodge the next day after being fined $8 and damages.

Drifting into Trinidad, Colorado, Masterson opened up a gambling concession in one of the town's saloons. Within a year, he was appointed marshal of the town. It was during this period that Bat's fame spread beyond the rough subculture of frontiersmen and he became a celebrity throughout the United States. He was visiting Gunnison, Colorado, in August 1881 and happened to be staying in the same hotel as a *New York Sun* correspondent who was at the end of a disappointing trip west. The reporter was in town to witness some of the six-gun violence with which eastern readers were so enraptured, but everyone in Gunnison seemed to be on their best behavior while he was making his rounds of the borough's worst establishments. Dismayed to think that he would have nothing to show for his tour, the reporter was sitting in the lobby of the Tabor House hotel with some recent acquaintances when he bitterly remarked that the wild tales coming out of the West must have been a bit exaggerated. Dr. W.S. Cockrell responded by nodding in Masterson's direction and saying, "There is a man who has killed 26 men, and he himself is only 27 years of age."

Desperate for a story, the young reporter dared not check the details of Cockrell's tale—not even with Bat himself, who was standing mere yards away. The article, "A Mild-Eyed Man Who Has Killed Twenty-six Persons," would make Bat into another one of the nation's frontier legends. Over the next few years, Bat was able to use his reputation to his advantage when he needed to. He bailed Luke Short, an old friend and fellow Dodge gunfighter, out of trouble with Dodge's authorities by riding into town with a self-appointed Dodge City Peace Commission. Masterson's presence next to gunfighters such as Wyatt Earp and Dave Mather was enough to bring the law to heel. Though Bat strongly disliked Doc Holliday, he intervened on behalf of the depraved killer dentist as a favor to Wyatt and prevented Holliday's extradition to Arizona on untried murder charges. In 1884, Masterson came to Short's aid again, this time in Fort Worth, where he prevented his friend's lynching by camping out in the jailhouse until Short was acquitted for the murder of Jim Courtright.

As he grew older, Masterson began shying away from the way of the gun. He settled in Denver in the late 1880s, where he owned and operated a series of saloons until he developed an interest in boxing that would take him away from both gambling and law enforcement. By 1891, Bat was thinking about hanging up his six-shooters for good.

Masterson had just married a singer and dancer named Emma Walters. He was also writing sports columns for *George's Weekly* and would eventually set up a large boxing organization called the Olympic Athletic Club. But Masterson would never be able to call Denver home. He made an enemy of Otto Floto, a powerful man in Denver's sport-fighting world, when their partnership in another venture, the Colorado Athletic Club, ended badly. Floto was a fight promoter and the sports editor for the *Denver News;* he wrote diatribes against Bat's Olympic Athletic Club, describing Masterson's fights as more fit for primitive mining camps than for the professional rings in Denver. Though Bat retaliated in his own weekly columns, his fight club foundered and it was not long before Masterson was on the brink of destitution. After an informal meeting in Denver's streets, during which Bat made Otto eat the gold head off his cane, Masterson sent Emma to her family in Philadelphia. He then went on his last tour of frontier saloons, turning a risky profit at the poker and faro tables in every smoky gambling house he could find.

Bat would return to Denver with his wife one last time to cast his ballot in the local elections of 1902. The poll watcher at the voting booth challenged Bat, and when Masterson protested that he had been voting at that station for years, the young woman responded by delivering a rather harsh beating to Bat with her umbrella. Turning his back on Denver–and the West–for good, Masterson and Emma moved as far away as they could from Colorado's capital, settling in New York City in May 1902. Denver would always remain a sore spot for Bat. Whenever anyone mentioned the municipality, Bat would cut the conversation short. "I don't want to hear about that burg," he would mutter. "To hell with Denver."

His experiences in New York were another story; Bat's latter years afforded him with a respectability and affluence that few gunfighters could boast of in old age. After many restless years on America's fringes, Bat had finally found his place in the country's largest metropolis. He got regular work as a sports columnist for the *New York Morning Telegraph,* wrote numerous reflections on his wilder years for *Human Life* magazine, and actually became a confidant and advisor to none other than Theodore Roosevelt, the rough-riding 26th president of the United States.

When the United States entered the First World War in 1917, Roosevelt proposed to raise a division of western "outdoor men" who would surely, he reasoned, give the German army a distinctly American brand of hell. Masterson liked this idea and, although he had become to old to throw himself in front of a machine gun, Bat suggested to Roosevelt that he and Tex Rickard, a fight promoter from Colorado, could advise the presidential candidate on "how to organize your European Expedition and how to win battles when you get there—you know Tex and I are wonders in matters of this kind."

Roosevelt's response was astonishing, bordering on absurd. Intrigued by the opportunity to hear whatever strategies the two men had in mind, he met the duo in his Manhattan campaign office. It is difficult to say what kind of impact Tex and Bat—two men who had no experience or understanding of modern warfare—had on Roosevelt, but perhaps it is fortunate for American soldiers that the ex-president never won another election.

With his gold-headed cane, finely cut suit and polished boots, Bat became well known in bustling Manhattan during the first two decades of the 1900s. By that time, his hair was thin and gray and his frame bore the extra weight of comfortable living. But his eyes still shone with a keen intelligence, and he bore his last years with a grace that suggested a remarkable life. Underneath the polished exterior, however, there was apparently a troubled intellect.

Bat Masterson was found dead in his office on October 21, 1921. Slumped over his typewriter, the last words he had written before his fatal heart attack spoke of a man beset by a guilty cynicism. "There are many in this old world of ours who hold that things break about even for us. I have observed, for example, that we all get about the same amount of ice. The rich get it in the summertime and the poor get it in the winter."

LUKE SHORT

5

LUKE SHORT

Luke Short was expected to stand up to men of violence on their own level when they came knocking at his door...whether he was working in Leadville, Dodge City, Tombstone or Fort Worth, Luke's guns were always loose in their holsters.

Whether you were a sodbuster, cowpuncher, hunter, miner or muleskinner, the common currency of the western experience was work. If cowboys were not driving massive herds to railheads, chances are they were slaving away on whatever ranch employed them. Farmers sweated through grueling growing seasons, hoping to make wheat spring from thin prairie soil. Miners labored long hours in dank, dangerous mineshafts. Teamsters, railroad men, hunters, homesteaders...for the most part, the western United States was a landscape populated by young men who knew little else but the relentless toil that dressed itself up in the trappings of American "opportunity."

Alongside the harsh existence of the western man grew another culture–the gaming society. A highly lucrative indulgence in humanity's baser qualities, the business of entertainment in the West offered relief from everything that was lacking in the hard lives of the people who settled the wild region. While most men's money was earned in a discouraging ratio to the buckets of sweat wrung from their backs, five cards properly arranged at a poker table could earn a lucky laborer more cash in a few short minutes than he might make in an entire year. If respectable women were scarcely found in the rough world past the 100th meridian, female company was available to anyone who could afford it in the bustling brothels of western towns. And when the burdens of dream and responsibility grew too heavy on a man's mind, there was always the freedom promised in the bottom of a glass, where all the cares that hung over the working day dissolved in the acrid brew of frontier whiskey.

So pressing was the need for these services that western saloons became the most successful business establishments on the frontier, and the sporting men who made their living off the dubious amenities provided by the saloons, gambling houses, brothels and vaudeville theaters became an indispensable part of the frontier drama. While the sporting man's bottom line was to make himself a tidy profit in whatever entertainment house he owned or inhabited, the nature of the business almost always entangled him in a multitude of other, frequently violent affairs.

Luke Short was one of the most renowned of these western sin peddlers. All of his adventures revolved around his single-minded pursuit of moneymaking in the shady subculture of gambling, booze and prostitution. Short was as calm and clear-headed a man as they came, much more interested in counting greenbacks than the notches on his gun handles. In this sense, Short did not have much in common with fellow sporting men like Ben Thompson or Doc Holliday, whose unstable temperaments made them poor businessmen. But commercial vice often attracted the worst men in society, so Luke Short was expected to stand up to men of violence on their own level when they came knocking at his door. It was a task from which he did not shrink; whether he was working in Leadville, Dodge City, Tombstone or Fort Worth, Luke's guns were always loose in their holsters.

It is likely that an extreme aversion to hard labor pushed Luke into his dissolute profession. He was only 16 years old when he left his parents' farm in Grayson County, Texas, and joined up with a ranch outfit that was moving its stock north in one of the late cattle drives into Abilene. Arriving in the roaring cattle town after several grueling weeks on the range, young Short knew in his bones that he could not endure another such stretch in the cowpuncher's saddle. But the thought of spending another year breaking ground on his father's farm did not appeal to the youth either. Suddenly all Luke could see were the limitations of the workingman—men who worked far too hard, as Luke saw it, for the paltry return they received.

Little is known of this period in the young Texan's life, but he was apparently impressed by the cowboys' festivities in Abilene. This is not to say that he lost himself in a debauched haze along with most of the other Texans in town. What struck Short was the amount of money that was exchanged in Abilene's saloons and how efficient the Kansan bar owners were at stripping cowboys of their hard-earned pay. It started when keyed-up cowhands arrived in town, intent on lubricating their trail's end celebrations with a saloon's supply of alcohol. Soon flush with liquid courage, many cowpunchers were tempted by the neatly stacked cards at the gambling tables. Cowboys, hoping to improve the wages they had just earned, would typically bet more and more of their hard-earned pay as their level of inebriation increased; more often than not, the establishment's dealers were able to win the money from their drunken opponents without too much difficulty. Those few who came out on top at the tables tended to celebrate by buying even more booze, at least until it occurred to them how long it had been since they had last a seen a woman. At this point, the bar's "soiled doves" would descend on the hapless cowboys to strip them of what was left of their cash. From the moment he saw the immoral racket operating in Abilene, Luke Short wanted in on the game. The rest of his life would be spent in the business of pandering to other men's vices.

Short did not enjoy a spectacular start. It took no less than five years of drifting through Kansas, peddling barrels of rotgut and learning the gambler's trade, before Luke was finally able set up his first business establishment. Actually, to call the dugout he carved into a hill on the Dakota–Nebraska line in 1876 an "establishment" is a bit of a stretch. Literally a hole in the ground that was camouflaged so the federal authorities might miss it, Short's "saloon" was more like a trading post where he exchanged rotgut whiskey for buffalo robes with wayward Indians of the Sioux Confederacy. It was a lucrative, if primitive, business: A gallon of Luke's home-brewed whiskey was worth about 90¢ in any frontier town, but the buffalo robes Short received in trade could sell for $10 each. The one catch was the federal prohibition against selling whiskey to Indians. Alcohol often had a destructive effect on Native communities, and one of the most pressing duties of Indian agents in tribal territories was to expose the white whiskey traders that made a profit from the ruin of Native bands. Luke made his money while he could, but it was not long before a cordon of federal cavalry troops rode down on his little operation and tied him to a horse bound for the federal prison in Omaha, Nebraska.

Short had no respect for any law that meddled with a man's right to make a buck, and he shook off the authorities during the train ride from Sydney to Omaha. Riding into Leadville in the fall of 1878–just as the discovery of massive beds of silver carbonate was making the town's mendicants into millionaires–Luke quickly established himself as a regular in the camp's rough saloons.

Nestled 10,188 feet up in the Colorado Rockies, Leadville quickly became a typical mining camp—coarse, hard and hungry—when fortune seekers began panning for silver in the surrounding mountains in 1860. By the time Luke rode into town some 20 years later, the camp had evolved into the silver capital of America, a rip-roaring mountain borough galvanized by the promises of wealth that the surrounding rocks seemed to whisper to its frenetic inhabitants.

The town's entire economy ran on the extraction of the shining metal, and the kind of businesses that thrived there says much about those who populated the region. The same town that housed five banks, three newspapers, three department stores and seven churches also supported 120 saloons, 110 beer gardens, 118 gambling halls and 35 brothels. Leadville was an ideal place for a professional gambler to work, but as Luke would soon discover, there was more to the trade than calculating odds, perfecting a poker face and hoping for the best.

Short had strapped himself with the cowboy's standard-issue Colt .45 when he left his parents' farm back in 1870, but until his visit to Leadville, he had never once drawn his weapon on a man. Luke's first gunfight came when he happened to be sitting next to the wrong inebriated man during a faro game in one of the town's gambling halls.

History has forgotten the name of the tough who provoked Short to gunplay, but he was a local badman who was reputed to have once killed someone over a game of cards. The type of person who was comfortable taking what he wanted and sorting out any consequences with the muzzle of his gun, this roughneck probably had no reason to believe that Short would be the man to reform him. Indeed, Luke Short was not a physically imposing man. Standing 5'6" with cowboy boots on and carrying no more than 140 pounds on his diminutive frame, Luke's appearance did not do much to inspire fear or respect from the physical men of the frontier.

Yet it has been said that the six-shooter was the great equalizer of the West—all a man needed to bring an adversary to heel was quick hands, steady nerves and good aim.

This truism was the last thing on the burly gunfighter's mind when he lost his last dollar while sitting next to Luke at a faro table. Reaching to Short's pile of chips, the thug was intent on having the former whiskey trader sponsor his next bet. But Luke was not disposed to random acts of charity, and he stopped the man's hand with a steel grip on his wrist. He did not even bother to look the thug in the face. "If you're looking for handouts," he muttered, "the church is just down the street."

The goon was taken aback by Luke's resolve and responded with a series of loud curses aimed at Short and every member of his family. Attempting to quell the imminent violence, the dealer thought he was doing Short a favor by yelling, "Gentlemen, please—rather than have this quarrel, I will make the amount of the bet good."

Luke was now guaranteed his money, but his principles as a gamester would not allow him to let this boorish drunk lay down a bet without any risk of loss. He tightened his grip on the man's wrist and hissed at the dealer. "You will not make anything this blowhard throws down good. That's my bet," he said, nodding to his chips stacked on the table. "Now let's get on with it."

Luke's assailant had heard enough. "Why, you little shrimp," he growled as his hand went for his six-shooter. "I'll shoot your damn hand off if you dare put it on that bet."

The conversation was over. Before the thug could pull his revolver, Short got to his feet and yanked the man's wrist so hard that the hapless rogue tumbled over the faro table, sending cards and chips flying. In another instant, Luke had his .45 in his free hand and jammed the pistol against the prone man's head. Someone screamed just before Short pulled the trigger and blew the man's left cheek off his face.

The badman's agonized screams filled the air as Luke calmly holstered his gun and bent down to pick up what chips were his. He claimed his cash from the establishment and exited without a word, ignoring the wails of the gravely wounded man behind him. Within the hour, Short was gambling in the next saloon down the street.

There was no arrest and no trial. Leadville's gambling houses were so crime-ridden during the town's boom years that the law could scarcely keep up with the number of shootings. Some reluctant marshal probably rationalized that at least the man had not been killed. But if the law ignored the incident, gambling hall proprietors did not. Little Luke Short was suddenly a widely respected man, and saloon owners were competing for his time during their busy hours to prevent the toughs in town from intimidating their dealers.

Luke was soon collecting a handsome salary from one of Leadville's biggest establishments while keeping a cut off the winnings at the faro table he operated. A few months of this work transformed Luke from a scraggly frontier drifter to the finely kept gaming man who would become famous. He got his long, bushy mane cut short, he shaved months of growth off his face, and he replaced his buckskin garb with a tailor-made suit and his Texan sombrero with a silk stovepipe hat. Sauntering through the rough town, looking every bit the Victorian gentleman on a sightseeing trip, only the hardness in Short's eyes and the shooting iron at his hip betrayed his rough origins.

Leadville was still booming in 1879 and Luke was enjoying his status as one of the town's premier card players, but he felt out of his element in this crowded mining town hemmed in by the crags of the Rocky Mountains. Short was a plainsman at heart, and he missed the wide-open horizons he had known as a boy. Besides, the gaming scene in Dodge City, driven as it was by the riotous celebrations of Lone Star cowhands, was being touted as the nation's wildest. Luke sensed that a profit was to be made from the desperate carousing of his fellow Texans.

Short arrived in Dodge City for the 1879 cattle season and got a job dealing faro in the famous Long Branch Saloon, where he made friends with two of the town's most feared lawmen, Bat Masterson and Wyatt Earp. Some historians have painted the working relationship between Earp, Short and Masterson as having been anything but lily white. It certainly cannot be said of either Luke or Wyatt that he was above cheating inebriated patrons at the tables for his own monetary gain; indeed, it was love of money above all else that drove both men in their western ramblings. But whatever the nature of their business in the Long Branch, Luke's association with the two law officers had profound effects on his gambling career.

Given the average duration that men of his stripe were able to keep still, the two and a half years Luke put into the Long Branch was a fair bit of time. He was the last of the Earp-Masterson-Short triumvirate still in Dodge in 1881– Earp had left Kansas for better prospects in 1879, the same year Bat was voted out of the sheriff's office–when he took up Wyatt's offer to deal cards in his new establishment, the Oriental Saloon of Tombstone, Arizona. For about a month, the Dodge City circle was reunited in the dusty hills of Cochise County, bringing the rough carousing of the famous cattle town to the deserts of Arizona. Short would have probably been standing right next to Wyatt at the OK Corral if he had not irritated Charlie Storms during a game of faro on the morning of February 25.

Bat Masterson had just risen from bed and was heading over to the Oriental for a little poker when he saw Short and Storms spitting insults at each other outside the saloon. Something card-related had the two men riled up, and both were on the brink of violence; they were standing no more than three feet apart, talking murder with their hands resting on their gun handles. Masterson was not in the business of peacekeeping while he was in Tombstone, but he was good friends with both men and took it upon himself to split them up. Bat took Storms by the arm and walked him down the street, suggesting that his haggard-looking friend had best get to bed because he seemed to be suffering from a bad combination of too much liquor and not enough sleep. Charlie mumbled something that Masterson took as agreement and accepted Bat's offer to help him up to his apartment.

About half an hour later, Masterson was on the plank sidewalk in front of the Oriental Saloon talking to Short, trying to convince the infuriated gambler that Storms was not so bad. But just as Bat was offering the olive branch on behalf of his friend, Charlie reappeared on the road right in front of them, intent on confounding his own ambassador. It was obvious that Storms' condition had gone from bad to worse; teetering on two unsteady legs with recently regurgitated vomit speckling his disheveled beard, he was staring at Short from beneath heavy eyelids. He groaned something that sounded a bit like, "Get out of the way, Bat," then grabbed Luke by the jacket sleeve and pulled him onto the dirt road while going for his six-shooter in the same motion.

To Charlie's credit, he moved quickly for a drunk man—his pistol was actually in his hand and aimed in his enemy's general direction when Short decided to shoot him. If such a thing were possible, Luke would have killed Charlie twice; his first bullet ripped through Storms' heart, sending the dead man reeling backward, and the second bullet hit him on the way down, blowing the brains out the back of his head. Wisps of gun smoke rose into the morning air as a cascade of Charlie's blood turned the dry ground around him into sticky mud. Short looked from the crumpled body on the dusty road before him to Masterson, who was staring dumbfounded at the corpse that had been one of his good friends. A few minutes passed before Luke broke the heavy silence. "Damn you, Bat," he said, then turned and marched himself to the marshal's office.

Luke was discharged on a plea of self-defense, but the murder made his presence in Tombstone a liability to Wyatt's political aspirations. Short was on the next train out of the county. He returned to Dodge that same year, enjoying a few months of casual gambling before getting his job back at the Long Branch in 1882. By February of the next year, Short made the jump from management to shareholder when he bought out Chalkley Beeson and became part owner of the Long Branch Saloon. Luke had no way of knowing that his newly purchased interest in Dodge's busiest gambling establishment would soon put him at the center of the town's greatest political showdown. And while Luke Short's name was already well known in many bars across the West, it was his role in the coming storm that would forever stamp his name in the tomes of western history.

While the chaotic carousing of hell-raising cowboys is the first thing that comes to mind when people think of Dodge City, the town was also a first-rate example of the type of corrupt political scene found in so many western towns. In a town where the leading citizens were business owners—and the most profitable businesses were saloons, brothels and gambling houses—there was no great demand for fair government. The city council was divided into two camps, loosely known as "the Gang" and "the reformers." The former was a freewheeling coalition of saloonkeepers and cattlemen led by the town's former mayor, James "Dog" Kelley; the latter was an opposing group of businessmen who ostensibly ran on a reformist platform, campaigning to curb the growth of the immoral establishments for which Dodge was famous. In reality, the town was run by two practically identical factions whose political differences stemmed more from competing business ambitions than from any ideological beliefs. Almost every town official belonged to one of the two parties.

Luke Short had first been pulled into Dodge's politics back in 1879, when he had become friendly with two of the Gang's most famous members, Wyatt Earp and Bat Masterson. Back when Masterson was sheriff of the county, Earp was policing the streets of Dodge and Dog Kelley was town mayor, Luke had been dealing cards in the government's de facto headquarters, the Long Branch Saloon. But by 1883, the power had shifted to the reformers' ranks, with George Hinkle in the sheriff's office, Jack Bridges acting as town marshal and Ab Webster holding the reins of the mayoralty. In April 1883, when Webster's protégé, former marshal Larry Deger, beat out Luke's new business partner and Gang candidate, Bill Harrison, in the mayoral election, the reformers felt they had finally won control of Dodge. So confident were the reformers of their power that they began a campaign to drive the Gang's leading men out of town—thereby setting the stage for what would become known as the "Dodge City War."

The war began on April 26, when the city council enacted laws affecting many of Dodge's saloons. Ordinance No. 70, "for the suppression of vice and immorality within the city of Dodge City," imposed fines ranging from $5 to $100 on any man who maintained a "brothel," "bawdy house" or "house of ill fame" and on any woman who was employed by the same dubious establishments. Ordinance No. 71, "to define and punish vagrancy," set fines from $10 to $100 for anyone who was found "loitering, loafing or wandering in the corporate limits of Dodge City without any lawful vocation or means of support." Men who visited, owned or ran businesses that employed prostitutes were also punishable by this law.

Despite the supposed moral integrity of these ordinances, it soon became obvious that the reformers' principles applied only to one specific establishment—the Long Branch Saloon. The problem, as far as the authorities saw it, was that the Long Branch was not only Gang headquarters but also the most successful bar in Dodge City. Dodge's former mayor and leading reform member, Ab Webster, was especially incensed by the Long Branch's popularity because it directly affected the business in his own "house of ill fame," the Alamo Saloon, which was located right across the street.

The law decided to do something about the Alamo's competition on April 28, when Marshal Bridges and city clerk Lou Hartman marched into the Long Branch and arrested three "soiled doves" who were on duty. Luke was initially unfazed by the arrest of three of his girls. Having been in the gambling business for years, he was familiar with municipal governments' practice of periodically fining their saloons to put money in the town's coffers. But when Short got word that he was the only proprietor who had been charged under the new ordinances that day, something ugly lit up behind his eyes.

Luke stormed across the street to the Alamo and burst through the swinging doors of the saloon. Sure enough, he immediately spotted Webster's two female employees plying their illicit trade. Short did not say a single word but strode back into the Long Branch, strapped on two gun belts and made a beeline for the jailhouse.

Luke's anger over the law's discrimination, fueled by his fierce protectiveness of his saloon's profits, turned his small frame into a tense bundle of violent force. There was no mistaking his state of mind as he swaggered down Dodge's Front Street, and anyone who saw Short coming was quick to get well out of his way. Lou Hartman's instincts told his legs to do the same thing when he caught sight of Luke bearing down on the city jail, but his unenviable duties as a municipal officer stayed his urge to run. Reacting more out of fear than anything else, Hartman stepped down from the plank sidewalk in front of the town prison and, with trembling hands, drew his revolver and took a shot at Luke. The bullet whizzed by Luke's leg, harmlessly kicking up dirt behind him. It was the only shot the city clerk made. Seeing that he had missed with his first shot, Lou dropped his gun, turned his back on Short and began a panicked sprint away from the man he had just tried to kill. As for Luke, he decided to suspend that old western adage about not shooting at a man's back and opened fire on the retreating Hartman.

If the following incident did nothing for Hartman's dignity, at least it saved his life: Just as Short pulled the trigger, Lou tripped over his own boots and went down into the dust chin first, knocking himself unconscious. Luke, believing that he had just killed Hartman, muttered something about just deserts and marched back to the Long Branch. Resolutely preparing himself for the worst, he kicked out all his patrons, barricaded the door, loaded his shotgun and steeled himself for whatever was to come.

Meanwhile, Hartman was revived out on Front Street and, after dusting himself off and retrieving his six-shooter, went straight to the mayor's office with news of the gunfight. Larry Deger and his men surrounded the Long Branch, but the mayor soon found himself in a difficult position—he simply could not persuade any of his lawmen to go into the saloon after Luke. The night passed with Short alert and resolute, staring down the ring of rifle barrels that surrounded the Long Branch. He was finally coaxed out of the saloon the next morning when a negotiator sent in by Marshal Bridges explained that Hartman had not been killed but had merely tripped when Luke fired at him. Short was told that if he surrendered and went to court, Deger would settle for a plea of disturbing the peace and let Luke off with a small fine. All he had to do was give up his weapons and go peaceably.

The sleepless night in the Long Branch had tempered Luke's anger from the day before, so he reluctantly agreed to Deger's terms. But no sooner had Short stepped outside, unarmed, than two lawmen jabbed him with the muzzles of their guns and marched him to the calaboose. Once behind bars, Luke was charged with assault and only granted freedom after posting a $2000 bail.

And then Luke was thrown into the jailhouse again the very next day, this time along with a handful of other gamblers who associated with him. When the men demanded to know the charges against them, they were told only that they were "undesirables." They were even denied the right to meet with any of the town's attorneys; when one of them wired his own lawyer in the nearby town of Larned, Deger met the man at the train station with a fully armed posse and suggested that the legal eagle would do best to stay on the iron horse as it pulled out of Dodge.

Encouraged by the ease with which he had been able to stamp down on Short, and spurred on by Ab Webster's machinations to squash the Long Branch, Deger took one further step. He was accompanied by a posse of more than 25 men on the morning Luke's cell was unlocked. The posse marched Short and his retinue of card players straight to the Dodge train station, and Deger gave the men two choices when they reached the tracks: east or west. Just like that, the gamblers were banished from town. Luke was scowling all the way to Kansas City, his pride wounded and the future of his saloon at risk.

It is difficult to imagine what Deger, Webster and the reformers were thinking. Even if state authorities did not intervene in this gross violation of the sporting men's rights, could the reformers realistically expect Luke to just accept his losses and set himself up in another town? Certainly they knew what kind of stuff Short was made of–and who his friends were.

A furious war of letters raged for the better part of May. One of the exiled card players, Tom Lane, sued Dodge City for damages. Short presented a petition to Governor George Glick, arguing that he had been denied the right to an attorney, had never been given the benefit of a trial and was a victim of "unlawful violence" that had been perpetrated by a corrupt government. Short concluded that a business rivalry had resulted in his being driven from his home and placed in mortal danger. The reformers responded by reassuring the governor that Dodge had never been more "peaceable and quiet" than it had been since Short and the other gamblers were banished. The reformers argued that Luke had been jailed for "refusing to comply with town ordinances" and later thrown out of town "to avoid difficulties and disorders." While Glick's respect for the word of law naturally leaned to Luke's side in the affair, he was hesitant about taking any action, given the dubious reputations of Short and the other outcasts.

As it became evident that talk was getting nowhere, Short began considering other options. Perhaps the smug advice offered by George Hoover provoked him to action. On May 7, a letter written by the Dodge reformer counseled Short to "either sell your interest in Dodge or else employ someone to look after your interests here and make up your mind to abandon Dodge, at least during the present administration." Hoover concluded by telling Short that this was "the only safe plan for both yourself and your friends."

Short did not react the way Hoover had anticipated. On May 13, the *Kansas City Journal* reported that "one of the most dangerous men the West has ever produced"–none other than Bat Masterson–had arrived in town. It was surmised, correctly, that Bat's appearance was related to Luke's troubles in Dodge, and rumor had it that a whole roster of infamous westerners whom Short had befriended over the years were ready to intercede in the gambler's plight. The confidence of Dodge's reformers began to evaporate as men like Wyatt Earp, Doc Holliday, Shotgun Collins and Rowdy Joe Lowe started arriving in town. The tone of the letters from Dodge to Topeka changed dramatically; on June 6, the following telegram from Deger and Hinkle was delivered to Governor Glick's desk:

> Our city is overrun with desperate characters from Colorado, New Mexico, Arizona and California. We cannot preserve the peace or enforce the laws. Will you send in two companies of militia at once to assist us in preserving the peace between all parties and enforcing the laws?

When Glick instead sent his attorney general, Thomas Moonlight, the resolve in the reformers' ranks crumbled. It was not long after Dynamite Sam, Dark Alley Jim, Three-Fingered Dave and Six-Toed Pete rode into town to swell the ranks of the gunfighters already loitering around the Long Branch that Webster and Deger capitulated and invited Wyatt Earp to discuss a settlement. Earp's only demands were that Luke should be let back into town and allowed to continue his management of the Long Branch unmolested.

The beleaguered authorities hastily agreed, and Bat Masterson escorted Luke into Dodge the next day. A number of the reformers' more zealous members left town for good soon after Short's arrival. The two ordinances drafted earlier that year were repealed, but for all the attention the standoff received, not a single shot was fired in Luke's restoration. Dubbing themselves the Dodge City Peace Commission, Luke, Wyatt, Bat and five other leading members of the Gang posed in front of a camera to commemorate their victory. It would become one of the most reprinted photographs ever taken in the American West.

After all the excitement in the late spring of 1883, that summer in Dodge was somewhat anticlimactic. With immigrating farmers exercising pressure against the migration of Texas longhorns–to say nothing of decreasing beef prices and the availability of new railroad routes to eastern markets–Dodge was soon past its heyday as a cattle terminus. Luke's enthusiasm for the Long Branch declined dramatically after the summer of 1883. Not only was the town's business community plagued by considerable unease after the confrontation that spring, but the potential for profit, which was always of primary importance to Luke, began a considerable downward slide.

In November of that year, Luke sold his interest in the legendary Long Branch and moved south to Fort Worth, Texas, where he began making the rounds in the town's lively sporting scene. By the fall of 1884, he had bought a share of the White Elephant, renowned as one of the largest and most opulent saloons in the southwest. Bat Masterson would later write that this was the most affluent period in Luke's life; all the years that Short had put into the rough sporting world were finally starting to pay off.

Never let it be said that men cannot change. According to legend, Short loosened his tight fist as he grew wealthy, attracting a whole retinue of professional sycophants who lived off his considerable earnings. It was in Fort Worth that Luke Short–the same man who shot a man dead for trying to take a handful of his chips in a Leadville saloon– acquired a reputation for generosity. One of the men who was drawn to Short's recently developed philanthropy was a local gunfighter called Longhaired Jim Courtright. A lumbering brute of a man who was said to have killed two men in Fort Worth and a couple more while drifting through New Mexico, Courtright appeared at the White Elephant in the winter of 1887, looking for work during a particularly lean time in his life.

If Short felt any sympathy for Jim and the family that depended on him, he still could not take the man up on his offer to provide security for his establishment. "Why, Jim," Short said, putting a consoling hand on the man's big shoulder, "I would rather pay you a good salary to stay away from my

DODGE CITY PEACE COMMISSION, 1883: STANDING (L TO R) W.H. HARRIS,
LUKE SHORT, BAT MASTERSON, W.F. PETILLON
SEATED (L TO R) CHARLES BASSETT, WYATT EARP, FRANK MCLAIN, NEAL BROWN

LUKE SHORT

house entirely. What with the way people around here shake at the mention of your name, if I pay you to stand at my door, you may well ruin my business."

Courtright did not take the rejection gracefully. He tried everything from bullying to groveling, but Short was adamant, and the big man left the saloon angry, humiliated and still unemployed. Unfortunately for everyone involved, Jim did not find work anywhere else either.

Early in the evening of February 8, Short was sitting at a table in the billiard room of the White Elephant with a few friends when death came knocking. A friend of Courtright's walked into the room and interrupted the conversation by telling Luke that Jim was waiting outside the saloon to talk with him. A flash of irritation played across Luke's face, but he thought it might be best to talk to the big man, perhaps to diffuse the anger that everyone in town had been gossiping about.

"Well, tell him to come in," said Luke.

"I don't think he wants that," came the reply.

Luke let out a loud breath. "All right, then, let's see what Longhair has to say."

As soon as he stepped out of the bar, Short thanked whatever god gamblers prayed to that he had his Colt strapped on that day. There was not much of a spoken exchange. Courtright–armed, angry and inebriated–lacked the verbal skills to adequately explain his feelings, but the two gun handles jutting out from his hips promised that he was more than willing to express himself in other ways. There was a short exchange of insults between the two men in front of the White Elephant, quickly followed by a sudden dash for their pistols.

Luke got there first. Brushing back his suit jacket and skinning his revolver in less time than it takes for a man to say "die," he fired and sent Courtright staggering back on his heels with a slug lodged in his ribcage. Fanning his revolver, Luke quickly added four more bullets to the bulky gunfighter's anatomy, and Fort Worth's resident killer was dead before his body crumpled onto the road. A deputy marshal arrested Luke right there and then, and Short might have had a close call with a lynch mob if not for the timely appearance of Bat Masterson, who guarded the jailhouse the entire time Luke was detained. Short's legal troubles were quickly concluded when the familiar plea of self-defense got him out of jail, and he was back in business by the end of the week.

The encounter with Courtright would be Short's last duel with a reputable gunfighter. On December 23, 1890, Luke was forced to pull his shooting iron on a saloon owner named Charlie Wright who decided to settle a gambling argument by laying for Short with a shotgun. Luke was hit in the wrist during the ensuing exchange; it was the only time in his life that he felt hot lead in a gunfight, and he made sure Wright paid dearly for it.

The rest of Short's days passed quietly. Living on in Fort Worth until 1893, the diminutive sporting man lived through the hazards of his profession to become the most famous gambler in the West. But if that was a distinction he was proud of, he was not able to enjoy it for long. After Luke had managed to dodge an untimely demise so many times during his frontier ramblings, death nevertheless took him prematurely by creeping up in the insidious form of disease.

In the summer of 1893, Luke fell ill with dropsy, a condition also known as edema, which causes an excess of watery fluid to collect in the tissues of the body. Short's doctor recommended a trip to the mineral spa at Geuda Springs, Kansas, but like so many of the medical remedies of the time, the jaunt to the springs was ineffectual. Luke's condition continued to deteriorate as the summer wore on.

His boots were off and his gun belt was hanging on the wall on September 8, 1893, when Luke Short took his last breath. He was only 39 years old.

BEN THOMPSON

6

BEN THOMPSON

Thompson crashed a banquet held by the powerful Cattlemen's Association, terrifying the toughest cattle kings in the country as he shot their plates and glasses away from them while whooping in diabolical glee.

Texans had one hell of a reputation. Whether they were rebelling against Mexicans, riding after Comanche and Kiowa, violently resisting post–Civil War Reconstruction or carousing in Kansan cow towns at trail's end, the worst denizens of the Lone Star State have been given much of the credit for making the Wild West wild. While many other men, women and circumstances contributed to the bullet-ridden annals of the American West, there is no other figure who stands out as prominently in the region's folklore as the Texan gunfighter. Men like John Wesley Hardin, King Fisher, Clay Allison and Bill Longley were the celebrities of the frontier, all of them well known far beyond the southern banks of the Red River. Feared and revered in every saloon, brothel and marshal's office from San Antonio to Deadwood, the Texan six-gun fraternity perfected the intolerant, short-tempered, dissolute behavior that defined the western badman.

Ben Thompson was one of the most celebrated of these Texan shooting stars. Cursed with a drifter's temperament, his mind was too unsettled for the work that most men put their backs into. He was a man who could not sit still long enough to do anything constructive. Whatever responsibilities he took on, from Confederate soldier to town marshal, were eventually undermined by a compulsive need for the kind of stimulation that could only be found in the darkest corners of American society. For the most part, his time on this earth was a blur of aimless days of wandering and whiskey-soaked nights at gambling tables, punctuated by the sudden violence that made western saloons famous. Thompson's one gift was his knack for walking out of those oft-lethal confrontations with his hide intact. Concealing an ugly self-loathing under a thin veneer of volatile bravado, the fearless gunfighter kept testing this gift for survival until it finally abandoned him in a vaudeville theater in San Antonio, leaving him a bleeding corpse in a room full of his enemies.

Was Ben Thompson born bad? Well, he certainly was not born a Texan. He came into the world in Knottingly, England, on November 11, 1842, but his parents moved to Austin, Texas, when he was still a child and he was brought up in the bustling young city. Thompson did not last long in the respectable society of hard-working Americans. His father, a disturbed rover, abandoned the family soon after they had settled in Texas, and the mild discipline of Thompson's mother was not enough to curb the wild tendencies of Ben and his younger brother, Billy. Ben was just 16 years of age when his cruel nature began to emerge; an early job in the printing trade was cut short when he blasted a boy full of mustard shot to prove his accuracy with a gun. Ben was convicted of aggravated assault, and by the time he emerged from prison a week later, he was no longer manageable.

Demonstrating a complete disregard for the well-being of others, Thompson got into two more shoot-outs during his teenage years, firing lead at people the way other roguish boys would hurl sticks or stones.

    He rode out of Austin as soon as he had the means and drifted into New Orleans in 1860, hoping to get passage to the gold fields of California. But the young man would never make it past the port city's rowdy waterfront district. Discovering the only work he would ever apply himself to in New Orleans' most lascivious neighborhoods, Thompson lost himself at the faro, monte, poker and keno tables of the city's crowded saloons and paid a high price for his education. It was while he was wandering the streets on the riverside after gambling away all of his money that Thompson would carve the pattern of his forthcoming days into the flesh of a man who had crossed him. Insults led to a knife fight, and Thompson left Emil de Tour to die in an abandoned shack on the outskirts of New Orleans. Ben was immediately branded a wanted man, and he fled Louisiana with the law close behind him.

    He rode back into Austin and was just beginning to make his mark as a professional gambler when the Civil War broke out. The same reckless instincts that had led Thompson to the poker table now urged him into the army, and he was one of the first volunteers in Colonel John R. Baylor's regiment. In some respects, Thompson might be seen as ideal material for a soldier; at 19 years of age, he already had more experience with murder than most of the other men that were enlisting. There was no question of his bravery where gunplay was concerned, but Thompson was as wild as he was bold, and it was not long before his complete lack of discipline made him as dangerous to his own army as he was to the enemy.

    Shortly after he was recruited, Thompson forgot what side he was on while stationed at Fort Clark in southern

Texas. Ben suspected that the fort's quartermaster, Sergeant Billy Vance, had been sending extra rations to his own mess, resulting in a shortage of supplies in Ben's outfit. Taking matters into his own hands, the impetuous young private walked into the crowded supply depot and stocked up on bacon and candles until he believed he had evened the score. Billy Vance came storming out of the supply tent 20 minutes later, roaring at the soldiers who were milling about. "What damned thief stole the rations of the laundress?"

While most levelheaded men would have kept quiet, Thompson loved the thrill of a gamble–cards or bullets, it made no difference to the foolhardy youngster. He stood up before the enraged sergeant and casually called out, "I'm the thief you're looking for. But don't fret over the laundress too much–I'm sure you can replace her rations with the extra issue you made to your mess."

At barely five feet, Vance was the kind of man who leaned heavily on his rank for any kind of respect in the rough Confederate camps. Tacking the martial crime of insubordination onto the theft, the outraged sergeant approached Ben as menacingly as he could, his hand over his revolver. "Now listen, boy, if you hand those rations over double-quick, I just may overlook your disgraceful insubordination."

Never one to be impressed by any kind of authority, martial, maternal, marital or otherwise, Thompson put on his best poker face. "Why, sergeant, I recommend that you come no closer, or you may regret it," he replied with an unnerving calm.

Vance responded by jerking his six-shooter, but–like so many others who would fall before the fledgling gunfighter–he was not quick enough. Thompson drew and put a bullet through the sergeant's chest, sending him crashing to the ground in writhing agony. A highborn Southerner named Lieutenant Haigler was stunned for a moment by the sight of a private gunning down a sergeant of the same army. Then, without a word, Haigler drew his sabre and rushed at Ben. Well aware that a private's life was not worth the brocade on a lieutenant's sleeve, Thompson hesitated for a split second before dropping Haigler where he stood.

While Sergeant Vance would eventually recover from his chest wound, Lieutenant Haigler was shot through the neck and died within the month. Thompson was thrown into the stockade after shooting the two men and would surely have been executed if he had stuck around for his court-martial. But if Ben was a man who courted death regularly, he was also the type who played hard to get when death returned the attention. Having no intention of sitting around and waiting for his funeral, Thompson escaped a month later after he started a fire inside his cell. As Fort Clark's burning jailhouse lit up the sleeping Confederate base, Ben slipped out into the night.

Thompson promptly reenlisted at another fort some 200 miles from Clark, and the rest of his military career was as undistinguished as its start was inauspicious. Much more interested in drinking and gambling than in the Southern cause, the wayward young man was determined to make a saloon out of every Confederate camp to which he was stationed. Drinking, gambling and brawling may have been scant entertainment in the face of the momentous forces that were battling over the fate of the United States, but it was the kind of entertainment about which Ben Thompson was deadly serious.

The only wound the gunfighter suffered when serving the Confederacy occurred when he was caught smuggling whiskey into his regiment's camp while stationed just outside of San Antonio. The colonel of the regiment was intent on keeping his troops sober, so he prohibited soldiers from going into the city to sample the local hooch. Ben, who was of the opinion that cards were a waste of time without liquor, had no use for his colonel's decree and was determined that his fellow Confederates should enjoy some of the spirits that San Antonio had to offer. Caught red-handed while escorting a wagon laden with barrels of the town's worst rotgut across a well-guarded picket, he set spurs to his horse and was soon tearing through San Antonio's streets with several officers right behind him. The chase was abruptly over when Thompson's horse lost its footing and crashed onto the pavement. Ben's leg was broken in the fall, and a few days later, he was once more under arrest—this time in a Confederate hospital.

Thompson escaped from the hospital in San Antonio as soon as he was able to mount a horse, and he was soon in the army again. The Civil War continued to rage, and as the monstrous battles in the East consumed men by the thousands, Thompson hobbled through Confederate camps in Texas with nothing in mind but the next poker game. In the small town of St. Bernard, he befriended Phil Coe, a famous and gregarious roustabout who was under martial probation for refusing to give up his self-appointed rank of lieutenant. The two men established a friendship that would last well after the war and went on a number of vicious drinking binges before Coe deserted the army and headed south for Mexico. Thompson went on a short leave, during which he married Catherine Moore in Austin. But neither marriage nor Phil's departure did anything to curb Ben's dissolute behavior.

During an all-night monte marathon in the Mexican village of Nuevo Laredo, Thompson had such a run of good luck that he had to shoot his way out of a room full of angry Mexicans, leaving two men dead behind him. Back in Austin a few months later, Ben got involved in a quarrel between Captain John Rapp and John Coombs, one of the Austin home guard's most notorious thugs. Thompson took on Coombs and his malignant posse right in the middle of town, and when the dust settled, Ben had two more notches in his gun handle. One of the men left bleeding in the dust was Coombs himself.

Given Ben's complete lack of direction during the Civil War, it may seem rather odd that he would choose to enlist in another army after the South was defeated in 1865. And yet the ink had barely dried on the Confederate surrender at Appomattox when Thompson lit south for Mexico to fight for Emperor Maximilian in the war that pitted liberal Mexican forces against the Austrian emperor's conservative throne. Like so many Southern men after the Civil War, Thompson was faced with a dearth of attractive options. The economies of the South were shattered, and while many Texans threw themselves into the cattle trade, the life of a cowpuncher was far too grueling for Thompson, who preferred indolence to labor. So Ben went to war in Mexico, expecting the same kind of lax routine that he had enjoyed in the Confederate military. Although Thompson did get into familiar six-gun mischief while serving as a soldier in Mexico, General Mejia accomplished what no Texan colonel had been able to do–turn Ben's guns against the enemy. While he was in Mexico, Thompson fought in more than one close skirmish and was even promoted to captain after distinguishing himself in the battle at Matamoros. He barely escaped with his life when Maximilian's army was defeated in June 1867.

Ben rode back into Texas after his two-year stint in the Mexican military. Once more in Austin, he no longer had the chaotic backdrop of war to keep his blood going–but the unsettled nature of western society during the 1870s provided more than enough stimulation. The last chapter of the American frontier saga featured Texan cowboys, gold speculators, buffalo hunters, hostile Indians; there could not have been an environment better suited to the young gunfighter's natural disposition. Meanwhile, Ben's little brother, Billy, was proving that he had no intention of being "the good Thompson." Drink turned Billy into a demon, and Ben–who was busy enough trying to keep himself off of Boot Hill–found himself sticking his neck out to snatch his brother away from untimely death on more than one occasion.

The year 1868 was a hard one for Ben. His little brother had killed a man in Austin after a quarrel in a local brothel, and Ben found himself up to his ears in bluecoats while he attempted to sneak Billy out to the Indian Territory. Shortly after Billy slipped out of Texas, Ben came home after a slow night at the saloons to find his weeping wife nursing an ugly shiner. When she confessed to Ben that her brother, James Moore, had struck her while in a drunken rage, Thompson flipped his lid; he stormed across the city of Austin and burst into Moore's home without bothering to knock. Before the inebriated man could slur any kind of profanity at Thompson for barging into his home, the glowering gunfighter emptied both of his pistols into his brother-in-law. As far as the authorities were concerned, this was the last straw. It was bad enough that Ben had made the Union forces in Austin look like fools when he orchestrated Billy's escape from Texas, but Moore was the third man Thompson had shot in Austin since his gunfight with John Coombs and his cronies in 1865. Thompson was arrested immediately after he killed Moore and was sentenced to four years in prison. Without any chance of escape, he would serve two years before the Reconstruction authority in Texas dissolved and Thompson was pardoned.

It was 1870 when Thompson got out of jail, and much had changed in the two years he spent playing tic-tac-toe on the walls of his cell. The large cattle drives had just been getting started in the spring of 1867, but by 1870 the enterprising Joseph McCoy had succeeded in making the Chisholm Trail the one major livestock route into Kansas. For about three months a year, McCoy's cattle terminus in Abilene transformed the small town into one of the wildest settlements on the frontier. Thompson was attracted to tumult like a moth to light. Although he cared little for the rough work of the Texan cowboy, he absolutely lived for the kind of revelry for which those same Texans were infamous. After bidding his family a hasty farewell, Thompson rode up to the Kansan cow town in pursuit of the gambler's tenuous fortune. In a sense, he would be luckier than he dared imagine.

Phil Coe, Thompson's old war buddy, happened to be drawn to Abilene in 1870 as well. The two men had barely begun to make their rounds in the town's saloons when they stumbled into each other after a night at the tables. If the experiences men share in war give rise to deep bonds, the same might be said of men in the throes of extreme inebriation; it was not long before the pair were fast friends again. Becoming inseparable in their nightly jaunts through Abilene's bars, they were the two most popular Texans in town. Coe himself was one of the great gamblers of his time. Endowed with an extraordinary talent at the tables no matter how many pints of whiskey he had put away, Phil managed to accumulate an impressive fortune during his wanderings. And even though he left scores of bankrupt men behind him wherever he went, everyone liked Phil Coe. A gregarious man who was known for his drunken generosity, Coe was one of the few frontiersmen who was more famous for his personality than for his skill with firearms.

Mostly using Phil's money, the two Confederate veterans opened up the Bull's Head Saloon for what would be the borough's last cattle season. As Texans began flooding into town in the summer of 1870, the saloon became one of Abilene's most popular. By this time, Thompson was as famous for his gunplay as Coe was for his congeniality, and the Bull's Head was stuffed to the rafters with pie-eyed Texans night after night. The atmosphere in the saloon was often somewhere between raucous and maniacal, but there was surprisingly little violence. Perhaps the wild patrons at the Bull's Head had a soft spot for two Texans who were doing well for themselves.

Or maybe they were afraid of the town's new marshal. In preparation for what was to be the town's busiest year, Mayor Theodore C. Henry sent a message of zero tolerance to any malevolent Texans when he appointed Wild Bill Hickok as marshal of Abilene. All men knew they were taking their lives into their own hands if they crossed the intemperate lawman, a Union war hero who was famous for his willingness to shoot drunkards, braggarts, Texans and just about anyone else. When Wild Bill paid the proprietors of the Bull's Head Saloon a visit and ordered them to edit their saloon sign—which depicted a bull's anatomy with a bit too much detail for some of the town's gentler citizens—Thompson acquiesced, and the bull's controversial parts were painted over the next day. Nevertheless, the same tensions that strained all Kansan cow towns when Texans were pitted against locals thrived during Abilene's last cattle season. Hickok was reportedly taking "protection money" from locally owned establishments, and it was speculated that much of the attention he directed at the Bull's Head was a result of its Texan owners.

Though there was very little violence that season, tensions between the Bull's Head's owners and the town marshal escalated throughout the summer. Things got a lot worse when Coe and Hickok began competing for a woman. Then, while Thompson was away on a visit to Austin, Wild Bill gunned down Phil Coe in front of a dozen Texans. Not a single one of them dared to draw on the marshal for vengeance.

Thompson and his wife were gravely wounded when their horse-drawn carriage crashed on the way back into Kansas, and it was while he was recovering in Kansas City that Ben heard of Coe's demise. Thompson was unable to walk, let alone go on the warpath after Wild Bill Hickok, and he sank into a deep depression while convalescing. He let go of all of his responsibilities to the Bull's Head, and the profitable saloon went out of business while he was floundering in a whiskey-soaked malaise that lasted more than a year.

Ben emerged again in Ellsworth, Kansas, in 1873. Ellsworth had begun to take over some of Abilene's business in 1870, and by the summer of 1873, the town was roaring with reckless Texan carousers. Ben got a job running a monte table in Joe Brennan's saloon during the establishment's peak hours. Despite the fact that he was in the rough town with his hell-raising little brother, Ben managed to stay out of trouble through most of the summer. All that changed on August 15, when the elder Thompson found himself face to face with a drunken cattle buyer by the name of John Sterling who refused to pay Ben a gambling debt.

It was not that Sterling lacked the money—he was one of the richest men in town, gifted with an amazing knack for winning any bet he put his money behind. And besides, Sterling made it clear that the issue was not cash; the issue was Ben. Perhaps the sloshed cattleman's financial success had so swollen his head that he believed he could take down one of the most feared men on the frontier. Or maybe he just hated Texans.

At any rate, when Thompson reminded Sterling of the small debt he was owed after a monte game, John's unfocused gaze registered somewhere between drunk confusion and extreme dislike. "Hell, Thompson," he finally answered, "I don't owe you a damn thing."

Sterling tried to get up from the table but fell back into his seat when his hand slipped on the armrest. Noticing that Ben was still looking at him, Sterling continued, "And even if I did owe you, I can promise you'd see none of it."

This time Sterling managed to get out of his chair and began to walk away. When Thompson grabbed the inebriated Kansan by the shoulder, he was treated to a sudden punch in the jaw. Ben's revolver was drawn and cocked in the blink of an eye, and Sterling would have surely been killed if policeman Happy Jack Morco had not intervened. The cop grabbed Thompson's wrist while the enraged gunman appeared to be deciding whether to shoot the pickled livestock dealer in the head or through the heart.

Ben got his cool back, barely. He spoke slowly, the muzzle of his gun pressed against Sterling's belly. "All right, Jack, you just take this man away and make it clear that if I see him in here again today, I'll do serious harm."

But not an hour had not passed before Sterling was standing in the doorway of Brennan's Saloon with a double-barreled shotgun and about a dozen friends; Happy Jack and a couple of other police officers were with him as well. Determined to play the gunfighter that day, Sterling yelled out his challenge. "Come out here, you Texan son of a bitch— we've still got some business to take care of."

That was enough for Ben. With an eagerness bordering on delight, he bolted from the monte table and dashed into the saloon's back room to grab his Henry rifle. Billy Thompson was also in the saloon when Sterling made his reappearance, and Ben's little brother quickly threw some shells into his breech-loading shotgun and prepared to join the battle. Whatever new headstones might have been put up in Ellsworth's Boot Hill were postponed when Ben's sloshed sibling tripped on his way to the saloon's exit and accidentally set off his gun. The sound of a shotgun roaring from inside the saloon had a sobering effect on the obstreperous Sterling. In seconds, he and his gang were running down Ellsworth's broad Main Street and into the cover of the surrounding buildings. The Thompsons, however, did not seem to be as scared of lead and strode out onto the middle of the boulevard. Standing back to back, Ben and Billy covered every one of their hidden enemies. Whenever one of Sterling's boys gathered the courage to try to take a shot, a bullet would send him scurrying back to cover before he could even squeeze the trigger.

This standoff lasted for a few minutes before the town's sheriff, Chauncey B. Whitney, appeared on the scene, cautiously approaching the brothers with his arms in the air. When it was obvious he had Ben's attention, the brave sheriff called out to the brothers, "Ben, Billy–what the hell is going on?"

Keeping his eyes trained on Sterling, Happy Jack and the rest, Ben told Whitney his story. The sheriff of Ellsworth was a man who ran his town as fairly as he was able, and everyone knew this. When he guaranteed the brothers safe passage to his office, Ben believed him and ordered Billy to follow Whitney. But no sooner had the men begun their march down Main Street than the unspeakable occurred: The drunken Billy's shotgun went off again while he was standing behind the oblivious sheriff. The depraved young man blew a hole through Whitney's chest, killing him instantly. Ben stared at his brother in complete shock. "For God's sake, Billy," he moaned, "you just shot our best friend."

Billy's face formed a hideous leer. "I don't give a damn," he snorted. "I would've shot if it'd been Jesus Christ."

Bedlam followed on the streets of Ellsworth. While the local Kansan population quickly judged their admired sheriff's death to be yet another example of Texan devilry, the visiting cowboys stood behind the Thompsons and helped Ben get his brother out of town as quickly as possible.

For his part, Ben made his way to his hotel room and waited for the worst. Legend has it that not one of the Ellsworth police officers could summon the courage to arrest the gunfighter. In disgust, Mayor James Miller ended up firing every last man on his police force and went into Thompson's room by himself to disarm the Texan. Ben refused to give up his guns unless Sterling, Happy Jack and the rest were disarmed as well. The Mayor agreed to Thompson's terms and peace was restored for the day. Ben even appeared in court the next morning and was released from all charges when Sterling's gang failed to show up.

But tensions in Ellsworth between Texans and locals continued to fester even after Thompson saddled up his horse and left town. A month later, a policeman named Ed Crawford shot down Cad Pierce, one of Ben's closest friends in Ellsworth. Soon after, vengeful trail drivers retaliated by rubbing out Crawford and Happy Jack. Billy Thompson was considered a fugitive in Ellsworth until he was captured by Texas Rangers and extradited to Kansas. The day the gavel dropped, Ben was back in Ellsworth, pulling every string he knew to get his brother out of prison. In one of the many bizarre twists of frontier justice, Bill would be acquitted for the completely unprovoked murder of the town sheriff.

Ben continued his rambling ways in the years that followed the gunfight in Ellsworth. He spent much of the 1870s gambling in rowdy boomtowns as they sprang up across the western landscape, sampling the worst America had to offer in Missouri, Louisiana, Colorado, New Mexico, Nevada and, of course, Kansas.

Dodge City was one of Ben's favorite locales. As one of the last great cattle destinations, Dodge was a distillation of the seediest elements of all the other cow towns from Abilene to Wichita. It was while he was roaming the streets of Dodge that Thompson became friends with Bat Masterson, the famous Canadian gunfighter who was serving as a lawman in town. So impressed was Bat with Thompson's six-gun prowess that when he was asked to write an article for *Human Life* magazine in 1907 and name the deadliest gunfighter in the West, Masterson did not have to mull it over for long before he came up with the name of Ben Thompson. Both Masterson and Thompson worked as hired guns for the Santa Fe Railroad when it went to war against the Denver & Rio Grande for control of western properties. Ben used the

$5000 fee he earned for his services to open up a string of saloons in Austin.

Thompson was in and out of his hometown throughout the 1870s. But even though he rode in occasionally to visit his wife, mother and children between adventures, the presence of his family did little to curb Ben's terrible nature. It has been said that familiarity breeds contempt, and when Thompson was having a bad night while carousing in Austin, the scant inhibitions he felt when on the road completely dissolved in the comfort of his hometown. There is more than one story of Thompson going berserk and making a shooting gallery out of whatever saloon he happened to be sitting in. When every glass, bottle, table and painting had been perforated, Thompson would saunter down the street to the next bar and do the same. Apparently he did not discriminate against his own saloons when he went on such rampages. On one occasion, he was especially infuriated at the way Loraine, one of his business partners, had decorated a gambling room in which he owned a large share. After Thompson had demonstrated his displeasure by shooting his own place to pieces, Loraine tried to get the police to arrest him. But as in Ellsworth, the local peace officers did not feel they were sufficiently compensated to go after a man like Thompson.

There were times, however, when the consequences of Ben's tantrums were much more dire than property damage. On Christmas Day, 1876, Thompson was celebrating the festive season over a poker table at The Senate, a saloon and vaudeville theater run by a man named Mark Wilson. Ben's poker game was interrupted when he noticed that Wilson was having a heated exchange with a ruffian by the name of James Burditt. Ben would have paid little mind to the confrontation if Burditt had not given a horse to Billy when the younger Thompson brother was being hunted by Texas Rangers about a year earlier. Not the sort of man to forget what few favors were granted him or his brother, Ben took it upon himself to come to Burditt's aid. By the time Thompson decided to get involved, a burly police officer named Allen had come at Wilson's call to drag Burditt out of the bar. Feigning pleased surprise when he bumped into the struggling pair, Ben pretended to be oblivious to the chokehold Allen had on the squirrelly Burditt. "Whoa, there, my good friend James! It has been a long time. Where are you going in such a hurry?"

Allen looked nervously at Wilson, who answered for Burditt, "He's going to the calaboose. We've had enough of this trash for one night."

"The calaboose? Nonsense," Ben responded. "I've been saving a chair for James at my table."

Wilson, along with everyone else in the saloon, knew that when Ben was drinking, any attempt to talk to him was likely to end in bloodshed. Wilson tried to be diplomatic. "Who is running this house, Mr. Thompson—you or I?" he asked. "Perhaps you should attend to your business and I'll attend to mine."

The Senate suddenly went quiet. Some of the patrons began edging for the door. It was clear that any more talking would only be a preliminary to the main event, which more than likely would involve shooting. Ben declared that Burditt was very much his business, whereupon Wilson responded by telling Ben just where he could take such business. Thompson swung at The Senate's proprietor, who nimbly dodged the blow, which connected with Allen's face instead. Burditt, now free, ran for the door, and while Allen and Ben were wrestling by the front of the saloon, Wilson armed himself with a shotgun that was kept behind the bar. His bartender, Charles Mathews, joined the fray by bringing his own Winchester rifle to his shoulder.

Shouts and screams filled The Senate as people went diving for cover or bolted out the front door. Wilson fired first, but he was jostled by the panicked crowd and his shotgun blast roared over Thompson's head. He was not able to fire another shot; Thompson threw Allen off and drew his Peacemaker in a single motion. Fanning the hammer, Ben emptied half his revolver in what sounded like a single report. An instant later, Wilson was literally dead on his feet with three slugs buried in his chest. In the same second Ben fired his third shot, Mathews let go with his Winchester but somehow missed, just grazing Thompson's hip as Wilson fell dead beside him. Shaking so badly he could not load another round with the lever-action rifle, Mathews jumped behind the bar for cover. But Thompson was undeterred and emptied his revolver at the wooden bar Mathews was crouching behind. One of the bullets found its grisly mark, tearing through Mathews' mouth and lodging itself in his neck. He would die of the wound within two weeks.

After the fight was over, Ben walked to the sheriff's office and turned himself in, claiming that Wilson had fired first and forced him to act in self-defense. He was ruled not guilty of murder and released the following May.

It may seem strange to us today that Austin's premier terrorist would be one of the leading candidates for town marshal, but in a time and place where a single man could turn an entire town on its ear, it made perfect sense to put that same man on the side of the law. Who would dare break an ordinance if it meant they had to deal with Ben Thompson? Because no lawman would dare mess with Ben when he was raising hell, it naturally followed that all outlaws would tread softly if the worst of their number was in charge of the peace. Thompson ran for city marshal for the first time in 1879, losing to the incumbent, Ed Creer. But two years later, Thompson's newfound prosperity from his chain of successful gambling establishments had done much to bolster his image. He now walked through the streets of Austin in a stovepipe hat and gloves. In light of Ben's newfound financial success, the town's citizens were inclined to forgive some of his past indiscretions and ignore the two Peacemakers that were still strapped to his hips. So it was that the gunfighter was voted in as marshal of Austin in 1881.

Ben was the town marshal for just one year, but by all accounts it was one of the city's most peaceful. While he put all of his energies into his new job, the responsibilities of the office seemed to steady his own disposition. In the entire year that he was marshal, Thompson was not involved in a single drunken brawl. Wealthy, well dressed and sober, Ben would eventually win the admiration of even the city's most upstanding citizens. It may have been the brightest year of Thompson's life, but like all good things, it did not last.

Ben had planted the seeds of his own destruction in Jack Harris' Vaudeville Theater in San Antonio two years before he was elected Austin's marshal. He had been in the middle of a week-long bender when he staggered into San Antonio's most infamous gambling house, intent on winning some cash at the establishment's faro tables. Half the night had gone by and Ben had been losing to the dealer ever since he had sat himself down. After a while, one idea lodged itself in Thompson's profoundly drunk head: The banker was swindling him. Convinced he was being cheated, the rash gunfighter refused to pay his losses and got up to leave. The dealer, Joe Foster, was one of the tougher gambling men in the state and went for his gun when Thompson stood up. But Joe was paralyzed by Ben's speed; before the dealer had even palmed his gun handle, Ben's .45 was drawn, trained and cocked. Thompson backed his way out of the Vaudeville Theater without paying a cent. Word of Ben's stunt spread through the streets of San Antonio, and Harris responded by making a public announcement advising Ben to keep his distance from the city for the rest of his days. He added that if Thompson was ever seen at the Vaudeville again, he would never get out alive.

Though it was uncharacteristic of Ben to let threats go unanswered, the years after the debacle in the theater were so eventful that he was not able to get around to resolving the issue with Harris until July 11, 1882, when he apparently decided that it was time to visit San Antonio again. Thompson took his children for a sightseeing tour of the historic city but had the good sense to leave them with friends when he went to pay Harris a visit at the Vaudeville. Walking into the saloon in the early afternoon with his hand on his holster and a belligerent sneer on his face, he learned that his bravado was a waste of effort when the bartender told him Harris was not in. Even so, he threw down the gauntlet with a series of insults about the bartender's employer, downed a shot of whiskey and strode out of the Vaudeville. Away from his duties in Austin, Ben slipped into his old habits. He took shots of whiskey in every saloon he wandered into, and by the time the brash Texan decided to pay Harris another visit he was roaring drunk.

Ben entered the Vaudeville, sauntered up to the crowded bar and took a few more shots of whiskey before again asking the bartender about Harris. "So, boy, any word on your boss and his shotgun brigade?" When the barkeep did not answer, Thompson continued for the benefit of everyone around him. "Well, tell him when you see him that Ben Thompson is right here waiting for him."

Ben did not have to wait long. Just as Thompson finished uttering those words, Harris was showing up for work. Informed of Thompson's presence by an employee who was waiting for him outside, Harris muttered, "I will shoot the head off that son of a bitch." He sneaked into the Vaudeville through a side door and made his way to his office, where he put two shells into a Remington 10-gauge.

Meanwhile, Ben was recounting his version of what had happened at the Vaudeville two years ago to a man at the bar. Thompson had not made it far into his story when word began to spread through the room that Jack was in the bar and that he had his shotgun. Thompson got wind of the news and was putting on an air of indifference when he spied the old bar owner behind the wooden latticework on a door that led from the barroom into the theater. Jack's silhouette made it obvious that he did indeed have a gun, but it was not trained on Thompson yet because he was still trying to single out the gunfighter from among the crowd of men in the room. Ben stepped out into the middle of the barroom and called out to Harris as everyone around him began a dash for an exit. "Hello, Jack Harris!" he bellowed. "What are you doing with that gun?"

Harris shouted his reply through the latticework, "Try taking a guess, you bastard!"

Before Harris could even bring his shotgun to his shoulder, Thompson fired three shots through the door, hitting the proprietor of the Vaudeville Theater twice. Jack was mortally wounded and would die in his home that same night.

Thompson surrendered himself to the authorities the next morning and made the usual plea of self-defense. Though he would eventually be acquitted of the murder in San Antonio, the incident cost him the decent reputation he had been building over the past year in Austin. Bowing down to the public outcry against his wayward slide, Thompson resigned his office as Austin's town marshal while still occupying a cell in San Antonio.

By the time Ben was released from jail, he had decided to completely give himself up to the demons he had subdued during his tenure as Austin's marshal. Throwing away his fortune in every saloon from Laredo to Corpus Christi, Thompson settled back into his iniquitous routine of drinking, gambling and bailing little brother Billy out of trouble. But it seems that something new began to worm its way into Thompson's psyche as well. It was 1884 and Thompson was approaching his 42nd year. The aging gunslinger's behavior was getting more extreme, and this trend was especially noticeable whenever he would come back home to Austin. The town's former marshal continued to shoot up saloons after losing enormous sums in reckless bets, and his wild rampages succeeded in scaring the entire Austin police force into paralysis. As he suffered bouts of insomnia that lasted weeks, Ben began to direct his ire at his closest friends as well as his enemies. One night, unprovoked, Thompson crashed a banquet held by the powerful Cattlemen's Association, terrifying the toughest cattle kings in the country as he shot their plates and glasses away from them while whooping in diabolical glee. He would also barge into the newspaper office and shoot up the type cases if the editor dared to run a story critical of Ben's escapades. Of all men, only Billy was exempt from Thompson's newfound capacity for hate.

In the morning of March 10, 1884, King Fisher stepped off a train at the Austin station. With an entire day to kill before the next ride for Uvalde County, one of the most ruthless cattlemen and deadliest gunfighters in Texas decided a little whiskey and cards might help the time pass. While wandering the streets of Austin, he ran into Ben, who was starting his day in much the same manner. Both men were famous in their own right and had something close to respect for each other. The pair had gambled together in the past, and if calling them friends was a stretch, they could certainly tolerate each other.

By the time Fisher's outbound train pulled into the station that night, both Texans were loaded and having a whale of a time. King convinced Thompson to ride with him as far south as San Antonio, and the duo resumed their festivities as the locomotive carried the oblivious men to their meeting with fate.

It was early evening when Fisher and Thompson arrived in the lively South Texas city. Not knowing when to call it quits, the pair decided on a few more rounds in the local saloons. They had visited only a few bars when the Vaudeville Theater became visible along the street. Thompson had not been in the establishment since he had killed Jack Harris, so he certainly had good cause to decline when Fisher suggested they go in for a couple of drinks. But Thompson was not a typical man, and he was not possessed of typical reasoning. In fact, the reckless gunslinger was probably thrilled at the possibility of a fight; drunk as he was, the urge to make some noise with his six-shooters was probably starting to work at him like a bad itch.

Fisher, however, was determined to keep things civil. He was aware of Thompson's history in the bar and had decided that it was his mission to reconcile Ben with the Vaudeville's new owners, Joe Foster and Bill Sims. Little did the two gunfighters know that the staff at the Vaudeville Theater had their own plans. Some of Sims' friends had seen Thompson and Fisher in town earlier that night and had run over to inform the bar manager of their arrival. Anticipating that Ben was the type of man who was foolhardy enough to pay them a visit, Foster and Sims set up a welcoming committee for the pair.

Sims greeted the two infamous killers at the bar and had a drink with them, talking congenially about water under the bridge and the nature of bygones. Ben must have been surprised, but he offered to meet Foster so he could bury the hatchet with the faro dealer he had drawn his gun on so many years earlier. Sims eagerly agreed and led Thompson and Fisher to the adjoining theater.

The two gunfighters would never make it out of the theater alive. Although there are differing accounts of what exactly transpired, it is widely agreed that a quarrel quickly broke out between Foster and Thompson. As King Fisher tried his best to calm the men down, the curtains of one of the second-story boxes were flung open and a group of riflemen opened fire on Fisher and Ben Thompson. Both men

KING FISHER WHEN HE WAS DEPUTY SHERIFF OF UVALDE CITY, TEXAS

were riddled with bullets and died almost instantly. They never even had a chance to draw; the famed gunmen's revolvers were undisturbed in their holsters when police appeared in the theater. Foster was accidentally shot through the leg and would later die when they tried to amputate it.

Ben had not realized it, but Billy had been gambling in a saloon across the street from the Vaudeville Theater when Ben and Fisher pulled into town. Drawn as always by the sound of gunfire, the younger Thompson brother interrupted his card game to see what poor man was being made a corpse over at Sims' place. His blood began to run cold as he heard the name "Thompson" being muttered among the men gathered in the barroom. Billy pushed his way through the saloon doors, and when he laid eyes on the grisly scene in the theater, he was stricken by something he had never felt before: heartache.

And so Billy Thompson stumbled out of the Vaudeville Theater and into the night. The depraved killer could not see anything through his tears, and as he wandered aimlessly through San Antonio, he was oblivious to the carousing Texans and the shouts and laughter that filled the streets.

7

WILD BILL HICKOK

*A pair of ivory-handled Colt revolvers...
became Wild Bill's trademark sidearms while
he worked as a lawman in two of Kansas' most
notorious frontier towns, Hays and Abilene.*

Jack McCall sat at the witness stand, restlessly shifting under the hard stares of those assembled at the Yankton, South Dakota, courthouse. The unkempt frontiersman had just finished stuttering through a grueling cross-examination, haltingly answering a volley of aggressive queries. Before the prosecuting attorney rested his interrogation, he asked one more question of the visibly shaken defendant.

"Why didn't you go in front of Wild Bill Hickok and shoot him in the face like a man?"

"Because," McCall responded, "I didn't want to commit suicide."

While McCall's name faded into relative obscurity after he was hanged for Hickok's murder, his inadvertent courtroom tribute to Wild Bill's skill with six-shooters would

JAMES BUTLER HICKOK, CIRCA 1864–65

go down as another page in the legend of America's most famous gunfighter.

A man who was as fast with his pistols as he was deadly with his aim, Wild Bill's legendary exploits in America's strife-torn West during the 1860s and 1870s put him in the national spotlight. By the time Jack McCall put a bullet through the back of his head in a Deadwood saloon in 1876, Wild Bill Hickok was probably the most recognizable frontiersman in the United States. Written up in countless magazine articles and dime novels, photographed more than any other gunslinger who twirled the shooting irons, and starring in more than one of the Wild West shows that toured through the eastern states, Hickok's aptitude for murder made him one of the first icons of American popular culture. But if the myths that were spun around the gunfighter turned Hickok into a celebrity in the East, the rougher regions of the American West made his legendary title into his greatest liability; Wild Bill would spend much of his time as a lawman and prospector acutely aware of how dangerous his fame was to his own well-being. After all, the West was brimming with badmen whose murderous careers depended largely on the scope of their own notoriety, men who would do much to add the murder of the country's most celebrated gunslinger to their sanguinary résumés.

Yet before he became famous as "Wild Bill," James Butler Hickok was just another young drifter on the plains. Not yet 20 years old when he left his home state of Illinois for the Kansas Territory, Hickok felt that same pull of adventure and opportunity that drew so many other Americans west. But the Kansas that Hickok rode into in 1855 delivered a heavy dose of bloodshed and heartache to determined settlers. As easterners rushed onto the plains of Kansas, they brought their politics with them—and the newly formed territory was soon torn by extreme sectional violence, pitting the anti-slavery settlers of the Northern states against the pro-slavery forces of the

South. By the end of 1856, 200 people had been killed in guerrilla warfare between Northern and Southern settlers. Rootless, armed and ardently anti-slavery, Hickok joined the fray, opening his powder-burnt chronicle in the brutal violence of Bleeding Kansas.

Although he rode with General Jim Lane's Free-State Army of Kansas from 1856–57, the details of Hickok's service in the famous guerrilla band are not well known, and it is hard to say what kind of role Hickok played in the merciless skirmishes that shook Kansas for two years. Legend has it that he so distinguished himself with his shooting skills as to become Jim Lane's personal bodyguard. Yet, for reasons unknown, Hickok turned his back on Lane's guerrilla army after a year of service to stake a homesteader's claim in Johnson County, Kansas. He must have already established something of a reputation as a gunfighter because the citizens of the new county elected Hickok constable of Monticello Township in 1857, the same year he arrived. All records show that James Hickok, all of 20 years old, was able to keep peace and order in his first bailiwick.

But Hickok was not imbued with a homesteader's patience, and he soon left Johnson County to take on the dangerous duties of a teamster. Hickok drove stagecoaches all over America's feral West for more than three years. It was during this time that he faced down several men who were bullying a wandering youth by the name of Will Cody on the Salt Lake Trail. When the dust settled, Hickok had won the friendship of the man who would eventually become known as Buffalo Bill Cody, founder of the Wild West shows and another one of America's most celebrated gunslingers. While working for the Overland Stage Company, Hickok was also reputed to have led a counter-attack against Indians near the Sweetwater River, bringing an end to Indian raids on stagecoaches in the Wyoming Territory. Two years later, he had his legendary knife fight

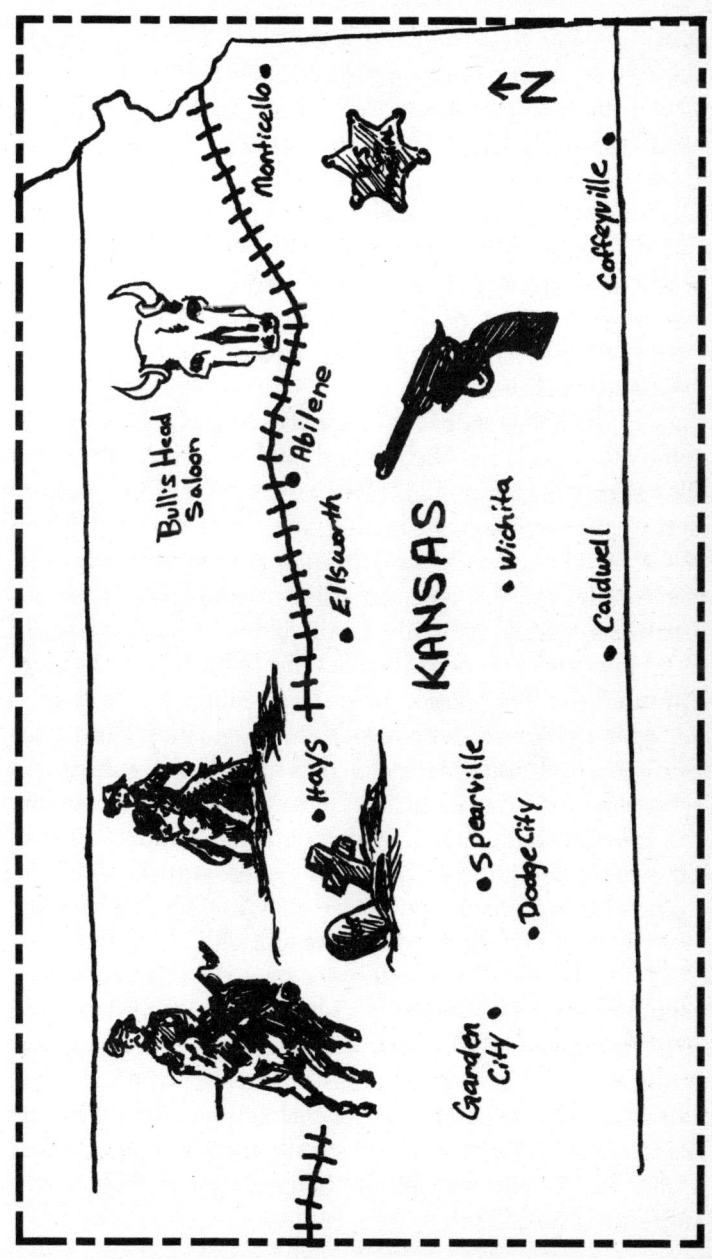

with a black bear while driving his team through the Socorro mountain range in New Mexico.

But it was not until 1861, when the Russell, Majors & Waddell Stage Company put Jim on duty at their Rock Creek station in Nebraska, that Hickok became embroiled in a feud with David McCanles and a legend was born. The bloody climax to the festering enmity between the two men made James Butler Hickok into "Wild Bill," and when the sensational writers of the time got wind of the story, they turned the solitary young drifter into one of the country's premier celebrities.

The first story of the incident at Rock Creek was written by George Ward Nichols and published in *Harper's New Monthly Magazine* in 1867. True to the tone of the western genre, the article was loaded with hyperbole. Nichols depicted Hickok as a superhuman protagonist who dispatched David McCanles and his brutish gang in a vicious battle that concluded with Hickok alone in a room with 10 dead men and a bloodied bowie knife in his hand. The story captured the imagination of eastern readers and was soon retold in numerous dime novels and magazines. With artistic license that usually translated as melodrama, subsequent writers kept adding embellishments to Nichols' tale; before long, writers had Hickok wiping out a bloodthirsty gang of 30 men single-handedly. In actuality, there was no McCanles "gang." Hickok faced down three men, not 30, and he killed only one of them—Dave McCanles himself.

McCanles was a wealthy rancher who had carved his affluence out of the frontier with the kind of hard-hearted determination that was common to so many fortune hunters in the West. A big and boisterous Southerner, McCanles was not above bullying, fighting and cheating to get what he wanted. He was a man whose strong-arm strategies worked well in his pursuit of wealth—until James Butler Hickok rode into town, that is.

It seems that even before Hickok arrived, fate conspired to pit the young adventurer against the town's boorish patriarch. Early in 1861, David McCanles had sold Rock Creek station to the Russell, Majors & Waddell Stage Company, agreeing to accept payment in installments over the next three months. It turned out that Hickok's employers were late with their payments to McCanles, and amid rumors of the company's mounting debt, June rolled into July without McCanles receiving a penny.

When Hickok was assigned to the stage company's Rock Creek station in early March 1861, he was still recovering from the bear attack in New Mexico. He arrived in town with a heavy limp and his left arm in a sling. If the obstreperous McCanles was the sort of man who enjoyed the debilitations of others, the fact that Hickok worked for Russell, Majors & Waddell brought all the ire the bully could muster on the young man's head. Throughout the spring and summer of 1861, McCanles took out his mounting frustration with the stage company on Hickok, mercilessly harassing the wounded man verbally and physically whenever Jim limped into McCanles' sight. Maybe Hickok, new in town and physically disabled, lacked the confidence to stand up to McCanles during those months, or maybe he was on orders from his employers to avoid confrontation with the man. Either way, Hickok took the abuse silently—but an ugly hatred began to swell in him while he nursed his wounded pride.

The tension between the two men took on a more personal tone when McCanles' mistress, Sarah Shull, developed an interest in Hickok. The pride of Rock Creek, 28-year-old Sarah had come north with McCanles early in 1860. Her passionate feelings for Dave McCanles had caused her to run away from everything she knew in North Carolina to be with the man she loved. Yet since they had arrived in Rock Creek, Sarah had been growing distant—and when Hickok rode into town early in 1861, capricious passion impelled her to notice the handsome, if badly beaten, newcomer. It was springtime and Hickok found it difficult to ignore the Southern belle's attention. In late June, when McCanles found out that Hickok had been paying Sarah Shull many late-night visits, he blew his top. The outraged rancher warned Hickok, with all of his usual bravado, to stay away from Sarah. But by this time, Jim's wounds were no longer bothering him, and he paid little mind.

To top everything off, it was 1861 and the crisis of Southern secession was quickly coming to a head. McCanles was a Confederate sympathizer and soon went about using his influence in town to secure supplies for the Confederate Army. Hickok, on the other hand, had been raised with the convictions of his father, an ardent abolitionist, and had already proved his willingness to fight for the elimination of slavery. Word got out that McCanles intended to confiscate the horses at the station in lieu of the late payments that were owed him and use them as mounts for a company of Confederate cavalrymen. Given his duties to his employers and his belief in the Union cause, it is easy to surmise how Hickok would feel about such a ploy.

It was in this environment of mounting tension that McCanles approached Rock Creek station late in the afternoon of July 12, 1861. He was accompanied by his cousin, James Woods; his 12-year-old son, Monroe McCanles; and a ranch hand by the name of James Gordon. McCanles was evidently not expecting much trouble from the people at the station, so he told the boys to wait at the barn while he went over to the station house alone.

Standing before stationmaster Horace Wellman's home, McCanles roared out a profane greeting, demanding to speak to Wellman about the money that was owed him. Mrs. Wellman came out to the doorway instead, addressing the towering man with a steady voice.

"What do you want, David?"

"I want to settle with your husband."

"He won't come out," Mrs. Wellman responded.

At this, McCanles took a few steps forward and gestured threateningly to Mr. Wellman's wife, thundering, "Send him out, or I'll come in and drag him out!"

Hickok appeared instead, staring with a strange calm at the man who had spent the last four months bullying him. McCanles was slightly surprised by the appearance of the young man at the doorway.

"What the hell have you got to do with this?" McCanles spat at the defiant form standing before him. At this point, the image of Sarah Shull came to his mind, and his scowl turned into an ugly leer.

"All right, then," McCanles drawled. "If you want to take a hand in this, come on out and we'll settle it like men."

There is a fine line between bravery and stupidity, and while Hickok may have crossed it a few times in his life, this would not be one of those occasions. Knowing full well that he could not last long in a bare-fisted brawl with a man like McCanles, Hickok did not bother to answer. He remained at the doorway, silent.

McCanles misread Hickok's silence as resignation. "That's what I thought," he sneered. "Now, boy, send Wellman out or I'll come in after him."

Hickok walked back into the house, where Wellman paced in fear at the thought of confronting the fuming man in his yard. The exact words exchanged between Hickok and his boss are not known, but when McCanles stepped up to the threshold, the two men were arguing and Hickok was holding his rifle. Hickok and Wellman's exchange was interrupted by McCanles' appearance in the doorway. The sight of Hickok enraged, with a loaded rifle in his hands, suddenly tempered the Southern man's behavior.

Nervous about letting the fight escalate into gunplay, McCanles broke the awkward silence. "Now, there, Jim, I'm parched. Will you hand me a drink?"

Something like a smile flashed across Hickok's face. Walking over to a pitcher on the kitchen table, he poured a cup of water and silently handed it to Dave McCanles. After taking a long drink, Dave turned his attention to Wellman, beginning to discuss—now in a much more subdued manner—the matter of his payment. Hickok stepped back behind a curtain that divided the front room in an attempt to calm his seething anger, but he found himself alone with his hatred for the overbearing Confederate tough who had harassed and humiliated him over the last four months. Wrestling with his loathing and a loaded gun, Hickok's rage mounted with every syllable that spilled from his Southern rival's mouth. McCanles continued to argue money with Wellman, unaware that these last moments might have been better spent in prayer of one sort or another. His angry voice was interrupted by the sound of Hickok cocking his rifle on the other side of the curtain.

"Hickok?" McCanles began, suddenly aware of how big a target he was next to Horace Wellman's slight figure. "If you have a fight with me, why don't you come on out and fight fair?"

With no response coming from the young man who was partially hidden by the thin calico curtain, the tension was finally getting to McCanles. "I said come on out—unless you'd like me to go over and drag you out."

Yet Hickok, still not interested in fisticuffs, finally responded, "You're welcome to try, but I'll tell you now, there'll be one less — in town if you do."

When McCanles made a sudden move for his pistol, Hickok shot him through the heart, killing him almost instantly.

Gordon, Woods and young Monroe McCanles came running around the barn at the sound of gunfire, just in time to see Dave McCanles, bleeding heavily, attempt to regain his feet in the last moments of his life. As the trio ran towards the house, Hickok drew his Colt Navy revolver, singling out Woods first. McCanles' cousin was shot twice when he jumped through the doorway. Woods fell back wounded and Hickok's revolver sounded again, sending Gordon reeling with a bullet in his body. Both men were killed as they tried to make their escape from the Rock Creek station. Mrs. Wellman crushed Woods' skull with a garden implement before he made it out of the yard, while two other men who worked for the stage company hunted down Gordon and shot him dead within the hour. Hickok turned himself in after the gunfight and was acquitted on a plea of self-defense.

The actual details of the shoot-out at Rock Creek may not have been especially heroic, but by the time Hickok rode into Fort Laramie in July 1861 to enlist in John C. Fremont's Army of the Southwest, word had spread that he was the man who had single-handedly wiped out Dave McCanles and his entire 10-man gang. Hickok, who didn't exactly go out of his way to dispel the myth that had grown around him, soon learned the value of a reputation.

Later that year, while in Independence, Missouri, Hickok—with nothing but his name and two six-shooters—waded into a mob intent on lynching a bartender with whom he was friendly. Pushing through a score of toughs that were about to drag his friend out of his home, Hickok drew both his pistols when he reached the front door and fired two shots into the air. The mob quickly went silent as they took in the impressive sight of the bold young man with his pistols leveled and his eyes flashing. Standing before the rough group of armed teamsters, scouts, soldiers and drifters, Hickok ordered them to disperse. The crowd wavered for a moment—a moment when any one of the 20-some men could have gone for their shooting irons—but every one of them to a man knew that this young man with his guns drawn was the same Jim Hickok who had reportedly killed 10 men in Rock Creek earlier that year.

Breaking the silence, Hickok continued, "If you boys don't skedaddle, I promise there'll be more dead men here than this town can bury."

That was enough for the men standing closest to Hickok. Only a killer or a lunatic would dare to pull this kind of stunt, and the clear-eyed man in front of them seemed dangerously sane. Seconds after the front rank melted away, the rest of the mob quietly dissolved and left Hickok standing alone in front of a throng of gawkers who had been drawn to the confrontation between the lone gunman and the angry lynch mob. Cheers erupted after Hickok broke up the mob, and one young woman in the town square was heard over the din of the applause. Perhaps mistaking Hickok for someone else, she called out, "Good for you, Wild Bill!"

From that day forward, Jim was known as Wild Bill Hickok and his fame spread among Union soldiers like a prairie fire, soon making him one of the best-known fighting men west of the Missouri River.

From the start, Hickok's attitude towards his own fame was ambiguous. At times, he was a barefaced liar, consciously inflating his own myth. When the famous reporter Henry Stanley interviewed Hickok in 1867, it did not take the journalist long to touch on the common yardstick by which all gunfighters were measured. "I say, Bill, or Mr. Hickok," Stanley stuttered before the towering gunman, "how many white men have you killed, to your certain knowledge?"

"I would be willing to take my oath on the Bible tomorrow that I have killed over a hundred," Hickok replied flatly. Stanley did not hesitate in recording this impossible boast as fact, reporting his encounter with Wild Bill in a newspaper article heavy with the flourish of adoration.

On the other hand, Wild Bill habitually poked fun at the absurdities of his legend. If he was drunk and men pressed him for stories of his adventures, Hickok would often embark on long yarns that pitted him against impossible numbers of Indians. These stories would invariably end with Hickok out of ammunition, his back against a wall as scores of enraged warriors rushed forward for the kill. Here he would pause, taking in the sight of his enthralled audience, breathlessly waiting for the outcome. He would not continue until someone broke the silence.

"What did you do then?"

"What could I do?" he would respond. "There were so many of them, all well armed, and I had only my knife."

"Well, then, what did they do?"

Hickok would give a long mournful sigh before continuing, "By God, they killed me, boys!"

The flummery of legend aside, Wild Bill's actual experiences were enough to make for extraordinary tales. Having come of age during the bloody years of the Civil War, he had been a sharpshooter in the battles of Wilson's Creek and Pea Ridge, picking off Confederate officers while entire regiments were obliterated by rows of riflemen and cannon fire. After General Samuel Curtis had secured Missouri for the Union, Hickok spent the remainder of the war exchanging fire in the fierce, if smaller, battles that took place in the West. The tales of Hickok's exploits during the Civil War as a sharpshooter, scout and spy for General Curtis' headquarters are innumerable.

As the war wore on, the stories of the intrepid scout's adventures—whether shooting his way through ambushes behind Confederate lines, narrowly escaping execution in a Confederate prison or intercepting enemy dispatches and riding through hostile territory to deliver them to General Curtis—circulated around Union and Confederate camps. It is difficult to know where fact left off and fiction began, but by the war's end, Hickok's fame had taken a life of its own and the flashy gunslinger was recognized in every frontier town he visited.

Not that Hickok made any effort to travel inconspicuously. In the years after the Civil War, Wild Bill relished his exaggerated fame and made every effort to cultivate his persona as a frontier hero. Standing more than six feet tall, he cut a striking figure in embroidered buckskin, flamboyant neckerchiefs and buffed boots; his long blond hair was always well combed and he sported a long, neatly groomed handlebar moustache that wagged past his prominent chin. Without a doubt, he must have turned heads in the rough towns on the frontier, where men had no need or desire to polish themselves up for each other. The contrast caused many easterners who observed Wild Bill in his brutish surroundings to dub him frontier aristocracy, and he was often written up as a blue-blooded gunslinger, the "Prince of Pistoleers," roaming among the frontier scraggle of America.

But to Wild Bill's detractors, he was merely a frontier dandy, and the end of the Civil War found the western territories teeming with ex-Confederates who were not at all impressed by the Union hero's flashy wardrobe. One of these Southern men was a gunfighter by the name of Dave Tutt, who was branded with a hot hatred for Wild Bill on the day his best friend took one of Hickok's bullets in the head during a skirmish in Missouri's backwoods.

The war was barely over when Tutt met up with Wild Bill in Springfield, Illinois. It was July 1865, and Springfield bustled with recently discharged Union and Confederate soldiers. If quarrels were frequent between the two factions, the notable lack of bloodshed in town at that time is understandable, so weary were the men of the extreme violence that had marred their lives over the last five years. Hickok himself would have nothing to do with the conflict anymore, saying, "When the war closed, I buried the hatchet, and I won't fight now unless I'm provoked."

Which is precisely what Dave Tutt did.

Along with most of the other former soldiers, Tutt and Hickok spent all of their time playing poker in Springfield's saloons, and it was not long before questionable gambling debts gave the Southerner an excuse to confront Wild Bill. On

July 19, Hickok was in the middle of a good run at the tables when Tutt approached him about a horse trade they had made over one of Bill's losing hands a few days earlier.

"Now, Bill," Dave began, his eyes red from drink, "you've got plenty of money—pay me that $40 you owe me for that horse trade."

Hickok looked up, annoyed at Tutt for interrupting his game. Without a word, he tossed his debt at the drunken Arkansan and turned his attention back to his hand.

But Tutt was not done with Hickok yet. "Now look here, Bill," he started again, this time louder, getting the attention of everyone in the saloon. "You owe me $35 more—you lost it playin' with me the other night."

Hickok had known for days that Tutt had a score to settle, but he was not eager to indulge the man's anger. Wild Bill swallowed hard before responding. "I think you're wrong, Dave. It's $25. I have a memorandum of it in my pocket downstairs. But if you say it is $35, I will get it for you."

Dave had spent the last few days gathering up the courage for this fight, and he was not about to be thwarted by good manners. He spotted Wild Bill's pocket watch on the table. "Well, regardless, I'll keep this here watch 'til you pay me the $35."

It must have been obvious to Hickok that there would be no easy way out of this now—Tutt was determined. "Dave," he said in a lower voice, "I don't want to make a row in this house, but you had best put that watch back on the table."

Tutt drawled back, "If you want it bad enough, you can meet me in the town square tomorrow morning at nine o'clock—I intend to carry it across the square at that hour."

As Tutt wheeled around and strode out of the saloon, Bill hollered at his back. "You'll never get across that place with my watch unless dead man can walk."

Within hours, the town was buzzing with the news of the exchange between Dave and Wild Bill. Knowing that his reputation would never survive if Tutt walked across the town square without a fight, Hickok was punctual the next morning—and so were half the townspeople, who were predictably crowded into two camps: Union and Confederate. The expectation of bloodshed made the spectators rowdy, and Bill stared across the square with focused attention amid loud insults and shouts of encouragement. When Dave Tutt appeared on the west side of the square a little after nine, a sudden silence fell over the entire town.

The sound of their jingling spurs rang throughout the square as the two men approached each other. They stopped when they were about 50 yards apart.

The silence became oppressive as the duelers lingered over their next action. No one knows how long they stood there, but all accounts describe Tutt drawing first. Hickok's reaction was lightning quick, and the two men fired almost simultaneously. But while Tutt missed, Hickok's shot blew a hole through Dave's chest. Wheeling around on his heels before Tutt hit the ground, Hickok drew his other pistol, training both of his revolvers at the dying man's friends, some of whom had already drawn their own guns.

"Aren't you satisfied, gentlemen?" Wild Bill hollered. "Put up your shooting irons or there'll be more dead men here."

Granted spare moments for reflection, Tutt's friends abandoned their impulse for vengeance and, after calling the gun battle a fair fight, sheathed their six-shooters. Out in the middle of the square, Dave Tutt watched his blood soak into the dust as Wild Bill's pocket watch ticked against his chest. He died before anyone could reach him.

Again pleading self-defense, Hickok was acquitted by a state jury. There was some controversy over the trial; Tutt's friends loudly protested that the jury failed to prosecute the defendant because the victim had been a former Confederate. Hickok did not remain long in Springfield to mull over the validity of their argument but set spurs to his horse soon after he was released from custody.

Hickok wandered west out of Illinois and spent the rest of the 1860s on the High Plains, looking for action wherever he could find it. In 1866, he was appointed deputy United States marshal and stamped order out of the chaos in Fort Riley, Kansas, where scouts, teamsters and laborers were on the cusp of all-out war with the soldiers who manned the fort. Soon after, Hickok went back to the military, serving as a scout for the United States Cavalry in the American government's first round of clashes with the Plains Indians. Serving under General Philip Sheridan in the bloody campaigns against the Kiowa, Cheyenne and Arapaho Indians, it was Hickok's task to carry military dispatches between the forts on the plains. It was dangerous business.

Spying on the movement of Indian bands and relaying the information across hostile territory, scouts' perilous duties were not envied by regular bluecoats. Countless cadavers were found on the uncharted expanse of the Great Plains, their scalps taken and their bodies mutilated. Often a scout's horse would appear–limping towards its destination, riddled with arrows, gore splattered over an empty saddle–as a horrific testament to the brutal end that awaited many men of Hickok's station. But Wild Bill's combination of luck and skill as a frontiersman allowed him to make it through nearly two years of scouting on the plains with his scalp intact.

It was while he was stationed with the Seventh Cavalry that Hickok made a big impression on the ill-fated George Armstrong Custer, who some years later would bestow high praise on Wild Bill in his famous book, *My Life on the Plains*. During these years, Hickok also became fast friends with General E.A. Carr's chief scout, Buffalo Bill Cody, who had come a long way from that day, years before, when Hickok had bailed him out of a scrape with a group of frontier toughs. Hickok gave writers more grist for their myth-making mills during his two-year tenure in the cavalry, and it was not until he received a letter from his sister Lydia on February 28, 1869, that he looked back to the eastern horizon and headed home to Troy Grove, Illinois.

Their mother had fallen ill, and Lydia, concerned that time might be short, suggested that Hickok should come visit. Hickok had not been back home since he had left for Kansas 14 years earlier. When Wild Bill rode into Troy Grove on April 3, he found his mother waiting at the garden gate, tears of joy gushing down her cheeks. In a moment, the most famous gunfighter in the West was in his mother's arms, being led back into the house he had grown up in.

If the picture of one of America's deadliest killers reclining in the security of his mother's home seems inappropriate, Wild Bill himself soon became conscious of how ill-suited his character was for domestic life. Whether riding alone across vast prairie oceans of wild grass under boundless western skies or drinking the night away in smoky saloons crammed full of swaggering rowdies, years on the frontier had carved their mark in him. As his mother's health improved, Hickok began looking for reasons to go west once more.

His deliverance came with a letter from Senator Henry Wilson late in May. The Massachusetts senator was swept up in the fascination many easterners had for the western territories and he was planning on taking a sightseeing tour of the plains. Having gathered a genteel party of Massachusetts society folk, Wilson found himself still in need of a guide for the trip. Like any man who would have read the frontier stories of the time, Wilson knew about Wild Bill's adventures in the West. The senator asked the legendary gunfighter to be his group's guide for their tour between the Missouri River and the Rocky Mountains. Beset by chronic restlessness and dwindling finances, Hickok jumped at the chance to be a frontier ambassador and left Troy Grove to meet the senator's party in Hays, Kansas.

By all accounts, the trip was a success. While managing to keep the group out of trouble, Hickok organized a five-week expedition that took Wilson and his friends through much of the territory that had been making so many headlines in eastern papers. It was probably during this tour that it first dawned on Hickok just how big an effect his legend had on urbane easterners. Entertaining his wards with drummed-up versions of his escapades and displays of exceptional marksmanship with rifle and revolver, it was not difficult for Hickok to fill the boots of the mythological "Wild Bill" about whom every member in the party had read. Hickok was handsome, well scrubbed and courteous; his ability to translate the gunfighter's rough qualities into a palatable package for milquetoast city slickers would eventually send him to eastern states as a showman. In fact, so taken were the New Englanders with their guide that they threw a feast in his honor when they arrived back in Hays. After making a speech in which Wilson praised Hickok as "one of the characters most essential to the settlement of the West," he presented Wild Bill with a pair of ivory-handled Colt revolvers.

These pistols would be put to good use—they became Wild Bill's trademark sidearms while he worked as a lawman in two of Kansas' most notorious frontier towns, Hays and Abilene. Hickok policed both at a time when it was said that there was "no law west of Abilene, and no God west of Hays."

Wild Bill was elected sheriff of Ellis County on August 23, 1869, and found himself faced with the difficult duty of taming the county seat. The young town of Hays, which had only been established in 1867, was growing fast when he was appointed as its peace officer. Serving as a base of operations for the buffalo hunters, skinners, teamsters and all others who made their living off the surrounding plains, Hays in its early years was as rough a frontier town as one could find. Whiskey, gambling and prostitution were the town's most profitable businesses, and nearby Fort Hays threw the often unruly presence of Union soldiers into the mix. Having become accustomed to a lack of real law enforcement after the town's first sheriff was killed late in 1867, the rowdy element in town was not especially pleased that a man of Hickok's reputation had just become sheriff of their borough.

For his part, Wild Bill was very well aware that his name made him a target to the town's ruffians. It was in Hays that Hickok would begin behaving like a bona fide gunfighter. Making it a point never to sit with his back to the door, Hickok always walked quickly whenever he was outside, striding carefully down the center of the street and keeping his distance from the storefronts on either side. Talk of his demise was everywhere, and he was constantly keyed up for a fight. He did not have to wait long for his first test.

While playing poker in Drum's Saloon on October 19, 1869, Bill's attention was diverted when the door swung open and the notorious Sam Strawhim swaggered in. A noted killer, Strawhim had been boasting for weeks that he would be the one who would end the pretty new sheriff's tenure. Naturally, Wild Bill had heard about this, and as Strawhim walked towards the bar, there was probably some part of him that wanted a resolution. Bill prepared himself for the worst, his right hand falling close to the ivory handle at his hip.

Strawhim evidently thought he could beat Hickok on a clean draw. When he was no more than six feet away, Sam suddenly jerked his Navy revolver–but an instant before he could train it on Wild Bill, the sheriff's own pistol flew from its holster. As the men at the poker table went diving for cover, sending playing cards fluttering through the smoky air, Hickok fired a single bullet through Strawhim's head, killing him instantly. This was his first contribution to Hays' Boot Hill, and there would be three more before a year's time had elapsed.

Two months later, a brute by the name of Bill Mulvey walked out of a saloon with a bad drunk on, smashing windows and terrorizing townsfolk as he lurched down the street. His biggest mistake was pulling his revolvers on Hickok when the sheriff tried to peaceably arrest him for disorderly conduct; what would have been one night in the calaboose for Mulvey became permanent residence in Hays' cemetery. Not a second after the intoxicated bully skinned his six-shooters, he fell face down in the middle of the street with one of Hickok's bullets buried right between his eyes.

But Wild Bill's most renowned confrontation as Ellis County's sheriff was still to come. On the afternoon of February 12, 1870, a group of soldiers had ridden into town from the fort and were raising hell at Paddy Welch's saloon. Not about to give any special privileges to military men, Hickok sauntered into the saloon intent on breaking up the party. Hickok walked up to the biggest and most boisterous cavalryman at the bar, tapped him on the shoulder and informed him that he was under arrest. The towering man looked down at Hickok before breaking into a wide grin and removing his own gun belt. The inebriated soldier then bellowed at the sheriff, "How much do you weigh, Mr. Longhair?"

"Only 165 pounds—when I'm in good humor," Hickok responded.

"Well, I hate to tell you, sheriff, but I'm not going with you. So unless you'd care to put up them guns and settle this like a man, I've got some drinking to do."

It has often been said of Hickok that, as a lawman, he used his guns too readily. While other famous peace officers like Wyatt Earp or Bill Tilgham would rather knock a man out and drag him away, Wild Bill steered away from buffaloing or fistfighting; it often seemed that he would just as soon put a man in his grave as in the pokey. Well aware of Hickok's skill with revolvers, the big soldier at Welch's Saloon wanted no part of a shooting match. By disarming himself in front of everyone in the bar, the soldier ensured that Wild Bill's next play was dictated by his own standing as a frontier legend; he simply could not draw on an unarmed man in front of all the witnesses in the saloon.

With a dark look in his eye, Hickok handed his revolvers to Paddy Welch behind the bar and asked the pie-eyed bluecoat to step outside. A cheer rose in the bar, and the two men exited the saloon surrounded by a ring of soldiers. As the pair quickly went to work in a harsh eye-gouging, bone-jarring, bare-fisted frontier brawl, the drunken soldier soon found himself overwhelmed by Hickok and crumpled to his knees. Moments later, five outraged bluecoats rushed Wild Bill all at once. Within seconds, he was bowled over and set upon with knuckles, boots, belt buckles and knives. Looking to even the odds, Paddy Welch ran into his saloon and managed to get Hickok's guns. Having suffered a severe beating by the time he felt the reassuring weight of six-guns in his hands, the sheriff released a one-man barrage, firing blindly in every direction. By the time the bullets stopped flying, two soldiers were lying dead and the rest of the gang was high-tailing its way back to the fort.

Looking like he had just gone toe to toe with a mountain lion, Hickok limped to his house and packed up his belongings. He was now a marked man with the dead soldiers' comrades and would not be long for this world if he stayed in town. That same day, General Philip Sheridan issued a warrant for Bill–dead or alive. Bluecoats were soon tearing through every house in Hays, looking to visit vengeance upon the town's former sheriff. By this time, Hickok had lit out east for Topeka, where he would spend the next few months recuperating at the home of deputy sheriff H.C. Lindsay.

Whatever the reason–maybe it was his inglorious departure from Hays, or maybe he was growing tired of bloodshed and wanted to try his hand at something more civilized–Hickok decided to hang up his silver star and would spend the next year in the unlikely role of entertainer. Recalling how Senator Wilson's party had been delighted by his frontier escapades, Hickok realized that there was money to be made in marketing the unfolding drama of the West and set about organizing a western exposition. Wild Bill put on his one and only show in Niagara Falls on July 20, 1870; he had mustered up three cowboys, four Comanche, six buffalo, a bear and a monkey.

The show was an unmitigated disaster. Hickok's little herd of buffalo got spooked when Wild Bill opened the exhibition by firing a volley of blanks in the air. After bolting through the stunned spectators and tearing over a nearby fence, the six buffalo were soon charging through a residential area. While Wild Bill and his cowboys galloped off to round up the stampeding bison, a troublemaker in the crowd unlocked the bear's cage. By the time Hickok returned with his buffalo in tow, his bear was ravaging the wares of a nearby sausage vendor while the monkey was pelting spectators with any projectiles it could get its hands on. If the spectacle was entertaining, it was not at all the sort of action eastern tenderfeet imagined when they thought of the West. To top everything off, Hickok could not charge admission. Because there were no grandstands or enclosed areas to hold his show, he was forced to rely on the rather lean generosity of the spectators when the hat was passed around. After counting the money at the end of the show, Hickok realized that he had come out about $1000 in the hole.

Too angry for words, Wild Bill was standing dumbfounded amid the ruins of his production when a curious English tourist approached him shortly after the show and asked, "My good man, are you an Indian or a white man?"

Hickok looked at the man blankly, then blinked just once before flattening him. "That's the kind of man I am," he muttered at the sprawled form as he made his way to a nearby saloon.

Wild Bill turned his back on the intricacies of business management and headed back out west. He would resort to army scouting again in early 1871 when an especially long run of bad luck at the poker tables pushed him to the brink of destitution. In April, a messenger from Abilene came to visit Hickok in Fort Harker. The cow town was about to enter another cattle season and was desperately in need of a gunfighter of Hickok's caliber because the town's first marshal had recently been gunned down. Jumping at the chance to get out of scouting, Hickok rode down to Abilene and was appointed marshal of the rough borough on April 15, 1871.

When Joseph McCoy built a 250-acre stockyard near the townsite of Abilene in 1867, just as the Kansas Pacific Railroad terminus reached the sleepy hamlet, he established what would be the first major cattle town in the United States—and the first municipality in the West to feel the roaring revelry of Texan cowboys at trail's end. Wild Bill was hired on as Abilene's marshal at a crucial juncture when the town's farmers were organizing to secure the rich lands around Abilene that had been used for cattle grazing. This would be the town's last—and rowdiest—season as a destination for Texas longhorns and the cowboys that drove them.

Given Hickok's particularly lethal approach to law enforcement, it may have been expected that he would produce a pile of Texan corpses during the cowhands' seasonal exodus. But surprisingly enough, only two men were killed by Abilene's marshal that summer. For most of the season, Texan cowpunchers quickly backed down when Wild Bill confronted them. By this time, Hickok had an aura of invincibility around him. He carried the weight of his past with a dreadful seriousness; while he no longer worked to foster his own legend, something about the way Wild Bill walked suggested that the man himself was even larger than the fables that had grown around him. Even notorious killers like Ben

Thompson, Jesse James and John Wesley Hardin chose to keep their guns holstered when they rode into Hickok's territory. So it was that the summer passed without much incident; although Hickok was vigilant as ever and keenly sensed how much the majority of Texan cowpunchers in his town disliked him, no man dared to challenge his authority.

It was not until October, when roughly half the visiting Texans had started back south, that Hickok's revolvers roared again. Phil Coe and Wild Bill had been at odds with each other since the stunning Jessie Hazell had arrived in town on August 2. Both men had designs on Jessie, and while she delighted in the attention from two of Abilene's leading men, her decision to court both of them set the stage for an ugly rivalry.

Phil Coe knew how to fire a gun, but to call him a gunfighter would be something of an exaggeration. Typically traveling unarmed through the streets of Abilene, the brawny Texan called on his own charisma, physical strength and uncanny skill at poker to thrive in the frontier town. He was a popular man whose jovial nature and good looks were complimented by suave mannerisms—when he was sober. Hickok, too, was quite good at putting on a polished veneer, but as the month wore on, Bill found that his marshal's salary could not compete with Coe's handsome winnings at the poker tables. While Hickok was detested by many in Abilene, Coe was welcomed by all wherever he went. Jessie Hazell slowly steered away from Abilene's poverty-stricken and embattled marshal, and by the end of August she was widely known as Phil Coe's mistress.

Hickok did not take this development well at all. While on duty one September afternoon, he got word that Jessie and Phil were at Drover's Cottage, Abilene's fanciest establishment. The news that Jessie was consorting with his hated rival seared Hickok's innards like a hot coal. As he stormed into the hotel in a jealous frenzy, the genteel airs that Hickok often put on around women dissolved in the red stew of rage and he tossed out a string of vile epithets. After he had finished throwing every insult he could think of at Hazell, he slapped her so hard she was knocked to the floor. Phil Coe, who was unarmed, did not dare utter a sound in the face of Hickok's fury.

Wild Bill next saw Phil Coe on October 5, when the Texan was leading a gang of rowdy cowboys through the streets of Abilene for the Dickinson County Fair. Drunk and intent on mischief, Coe fired his revolver into the air, goading the boys around him into howling with glee. Not a moment later, Hickok came running out of the Alamo Saloon, taking in the sight of Coe with his band of revelers and the smoking gun still in his enemy's hand. The Texans suddenly got very, very quiet.

"Who fired that shot?" Hickok demanded, staring directly at the man he intended to punish.

Coe had no skill with a six-shooter; to his credit, he knew it. Maybe if he had not been saturated with rotgut whiskey, he would have had the sense to defer to Wild Bill. But standing there in front of all those men, the showman in him came out.

Flashing a toothy grin, Phil replied, "I did."

"Why?"

"I was shooting at a mad dog."

Coe's friends broke into laughter, shouting encouragement at their fellow Texan. Wild Bill, however, was not amused. The gunfighter saw an enemy with a loaded gun in his hands—no cause for jest. Hickok's hands slowly made their way to the handles of his holstered revolvers. Noticing Hickok's movement, Phil Coe panicked. He raised his gun and fired, managing to completely miss Hickok, who stood no more than 10 feet away. Wild Bill had his guns out even before Coe got his shot off. A split second after the Texan fired, he had two slugs in his stomach and was writhing in bloody agony before the shocked cowboys.

Turning on the crowd, Wild Bill roared, "If any of you want the balance of these pills, come and get them."

There was only stunned silence.

Hickok continued, "Now every one of you mount a pony and ride for your camp. And do it damn quick!"

It was then that Bill saw in the corner of his eye the form of a man moving rapidly toward him. Acting purely on reflex, Hickok spun and fired, assuming that the man was a Texan intent on avenging Coe. Wild Bill's blood went cold when he instead saw one of his deputies; Mike Williams crumpled to the ground with eyes staring in mute shock at the starry sky and two bullet holes in his forehead. Williams had apparently come running to the scene after he heard the exchange of gunfire, hoping to assist the sheriff in dealing with the rest of the cowpunchers. It was the first time that Hickok's much-lauded reflexes worked against him, and it is said that he lapsed into a deep grief for a long time afterward. Williams was the last man Wild Bill would ever kill.

Hickok was discharged from duty at Abilene after the last of the Texans departed, and for the most part he spent the rest of his years drifting aimlessly. Wandering from town to town, he languished in saloons for days on end, drinking heavily and playing cards. His love for gambling was not accompanied by any kind of real skill, and he was known to go on costly losing streaks. After meeting up with his old friend Buffalo Bill Cody in 1873, Hickok was lured into acting for Cody's "Scouts of the Prairie" Wild West Show. Unlike Hickok's own attempt at this business three years earlier, Buffalo Bill's exhibition was a resounding success. After years of touring through the United States, Cody would go on to take his show to Europe; as late as 1903, he was still attracting international audiences to his famous Wild West Shows.

Unfortunately, Wild Bill did not prove to be a good actor. Conscious of the unintentional parody in which the melodramatic script and clumsy props cast him and his kind,

Hickok insisted to Buffalo Bill that he and his troupe were making fools of themselves, "becoming the laughingstock of the people." After bitterly leaving eastern stages behind in 1874, Hickok rode west for the last time, settling for a while in Cheyenne, Wyoming Territory, where he would marry a woman by the name of Agnes Lake.

Confronted with the responsibilities of domestic life, Hickok began thinking about making a good living. Drawn by news of gold in the Black Hills in 1876, he departed for Deadwood, South Dakota, confident that he could make some good money as a mine owner. It was in that lawless mining camp that Wild Bill would meet his end.

In light of the grand scope of Hickok's adventures—a spectacular string of events that took him from fighting in the Civil War to dodging war bands in hostile Indian Territory to serving as a lawman in two of Kansas' most dangerous boroughs—we might expect that his death would be at least as striking as his life had been. But Hickok was not destined to go down in a blaze of glory.

Sitting at a poker table in the No. 10 Saloon on August 2, 1876, Hickok paid no mind when a scraggly drifter by the name of Jack McCall strolled into the bar. McCall, whose motive would never be revealed, walked as casually as he could to where Hickok was sitting and calmly shot Wild Bill through the back of the head. The famed gunfighter died without a sound, blasted into oblivion at age 39 by a man who had never drawn a gun on anyone before. So sparse was the drama in Hickok's death that storytellers turned to the cards he held in his last moments to divine some kind of significance from the event. So it was that the two black aces and two black eights Hickok held in the last moments of his life became known from that day forward as the "dead man's hand." After revealing no purpose for the murder during his trial a year later, Jack McCall was hanged on March 1, 1877.

8

CHARLIE SIRINGO

Before Siringo had time to figure out a plan, the mob came storming back into town. The detective was quickly surrounded by men who were glowering at him from behind cocked guns.

Sitting at a desk at the back of his cigar shop in Caldwell, Kansas, Charlie Siringo stared at the blank sheet of paper that lay before him. You would have had to look closely to notice the signs that set him apart from other tobacco merchants. He was dressed in the customary starched shirt, tie and freshly cleaned trousers, but his hands were not those of a man who made his living behind a shopkeeper's desk. Notched, gnarled and callused, they bore the mark of every mustang or steer he had ever roped, wrestled or branded. Deep furrows ran down his weather-beaten face, betraying years spent living in the saddle under a blistering Texas sun, watching over vast herds of bad-tempered longhorns. And the light that shone behind his sharp gray eyes suggested a vigorous character, developed by the remarkable experiences of working as a cowboy during

CHARLIE SIRINGO AS A YOUNG MAN

the golden age of the American cattle industry. Shifting uncomfortably in his chair, Charlie frowned again at the paper on his desk before hunching forward to pen the title of his first written work:

> *A Texas Cow Boy, or, Fifteen Years on the Hurricane Deck of a Spanish Pony. Taken From Real Life by Chas. A. Siringo, an Old Stove Up "Cow Puncher" Who Has Spent Nearly Twenty Years on the Great Western Cattle Ranches.*

The year was 1884, and 12 months had gone by since Siringo–who was not yet 30 years old–had sworn off the rough, rootless work of cowpunching. Settling in Caldwell, Kansas, with his young bride, Mamie Lloyd, Siringo hung up his wide-brimmed cowboy hat, chaps and revolver, intent on a sedentary life in the bustling young frontier town. Yet try as he might, Charlie could not shake the Texas dust from his boots or the freewheeling cowboy life from his mind, and he was soon seeking an outlet for the wanderlust that 15 years on the open range had driven into him.

Surprisingly enough, Siringo did not turn to the frontier's most common painkillers, whiskey and cards. A pensive man by nature, he turned his nostalgic longing inward and sat down to write what would be the first autobiography of a cowboy. The finished work, *A Texas Cow Boy*, was published in 1885 and was an instant success; it eventually sold close to a million copies and became a western classic. Pandering to an eastern readership that was fascinated by the frontier, the non-fictional account of life on the open range gave readers a precise, if somewhat dramatized, look at "business as usual" as it occurred on the sprawling cattle empires in the West. Up until 1883, the cowboy way had been the only life Charlie Siringo had ever known.

Born on February 7, 1855, on the Matagorda Peninsula in southeast Texas, Siringo came of age in a region that had become known as the "cradle of the cattle kingdom": Lush grasslands, abundant water and scarce predators allowed longhorns to flourish. The peninsula itself was covered with free-roaming cattle, and Siringo grew up among the rangy animals. Helping his widowed mother on her small ranch, he roped and rode calves while his mother did the milking. By the time he was 12 years old, Siringo was rounding up 1000-pound mavericks for branding. A few years later, the wiry little adolescent was breaking wild horses at $2.50 a head–dangerous work that even the most experienced cowhands shied away from. Over the next decade and a half, Siringo's life was tightly bound to the cattle industry. From working as a ranch hand on Shanghai Pierce's Rancho Grande to establishing the LX Ranch on the Texas Panhandle to driving thousands of longhorns up the Chisholm Trail into Kansas, Charlie Siringo was involved with every kind of work that a cowboy could take on.

But the open range did not last long. Texas cattle country was soon overpopulated, overgrazed and fenced in, and westward-moving farmers began to compete with cattlemen for the ever-dwindling land. As these pressures led to increased conflict, the face of the cattle industry began to change. By the mid-1880s, fenced plains made the massive trail drives of the 1870s impossible, and the newly enclosed ranches transformed the cattle-driving cowboy into the stationary ranch hand. Though he had become an expert cattleman, Siringo did not like the new order of things, and in 1883 he gave up his job as top hand on the LX Company's ranch just south of Caldwell.

No longer a cowboy by trade, Siringo would always be a cowboy at heart–and he was not able to last long in the sedentary routine of urban life. Shortly after *A Texas Cow Boy* was published, he sold his cigar shop, loaded up his wagon and moved to lively Chicago with his wife. In the second edition of *A Texas Cow Boy*, Siringo boasted that his move to Chicago was largely driven by financial ambition in the promotion of his successful book. But given the nature of the work he would soon fall into, it is obvious that Siringo had not taken well to shopkeeping and that his move was motivated by an itch for excitement just as much as it was for money.

Charlie and Mamie had not been in Chicago for a week when anarchists hurled the bomb that inspired Siringo to take up a new career. When the smoke cleared after the Haymarket Square riot, seven officers were dead and 67 were wounded. Though Mamie did not allow Charlie to go out the night the bomb shook the house they were boarding in, she was not able to stop her adventurous husband from eventually getting involved. Three months later, Siringo was sitting before William A. Pinkerton at the head office of the Pinkerton Detective Agency, applying for work "so as to help ferret out the thrower of the bomb and his backers."

Siringo's experiences with law enforcement were limited, to say the least. In 1880, he had led a vigilante outfit into New Mexico in search of cattle that Billy the Kid's gang had stolen from the LX Company on the Texas Panhandle. Though he was given orders to capture the rustlers if he could find them, his main purpose was to get back as many cattle as he could. Siringo's seven-month odyssey took him through much of New Mexico, herding together LX cattle as he found them. While he did have encounters with Pat Garrett and was for a time close on the trail of Billy the Kid, Siringo did not capture a single cattle thief. But William Pinkerton liked what he saw, and Siringo was promptly hired on by America's most famous private detective company.

Working on the Haymarket affair for the first few months of his employment, Siringo witnessed how heavy-handed the Pinkertons could be if they had to be. Not about to let such an extreme attack go unpunished, the authorities went about seeking vengeance with a fierce determination, and the Pinkerton Detective Agency was hired to hasten the judicial process. Siringo would later write that the Pinkerton company was paid to fabricate evidence in the conviction of eight anarchists who stood trial for the bombing—and that the jury had been fixed for the prosecution. Of the eight defendants, four were hanged, one committed suicide in prison, and Governor John Altgeld pardoned the three remaining men in 1893, stating that the prisoners had been victims of "malicious ferocity."

But the Pinkerton way was to get their man, and if Siringo was troubled by the agency's ferocious or relentless methods, he was not overly so. He told himself that even though the justice had been corrupt, the end justified the means. Believing foreign-born anarchists to be the curse of American society, Charlie endowed his inborn sense of adventure with a political purpose and threw himself into his work with an extraordinary zeal. His career with the Pinkertons would be spectacular. Siringo worked for the agency for more than 20 years, and his assignments took him all over the United States—hunting gold thieves through frigid Alaskan inlets, infiltrating labor unions during the Coeur d'Alene labor riots of 1892 and chasing down Butch Cassidy's band of renegades. Charlie would have more than enough adventures to boast of in another book.

During the summer of 1886, however, sitting down to write again was the furthest thing from Charlie's mind. The Pinkerton Detective Agency had just reassigned Siringo to its Denver office. Having never really adjusted to city life in Chicago, Siringo and his wife were glad to be back on "their" side of the Mississippi River. The wide-open territory of the West was where Siringo belonged. It was in Pinkerton's Denver office, under the supervision of James McParland,

CHARLIE SIRINGO, PINKERTON AGENT

that Siringo would become the famous self-proclaimed "cowboy detective." His ability to go long distances in the saddle over tough terrain in the ugliest kind of weather–talents he picked up during his days as a cattleman–made him the best manhunter in the Pinkerton agency. If his career as a detective was not particularly honest, honorable or rewarding, at least it gave the natural born raconteur more material for the ongoing story of his life.

  Siringo got his first big assignment in early spring of 1887, when political violence flared up in Archuleta County on Colorado's southwest border. Tired of the Archuleta family's stranglehold on the reins of power in the county seat, a group of so-called anarchists chased out the ruling clan after the Archuletas had won another crooked election. The problem was that the Archuleta family was in the habit of bringing their New Mexico shepherds in from the other side of border to vote whenever a county election was held. In 1887, the citizens of the county finally took the law into their own hands, wished the Archuletas happy trails with the muzzles of their guns and seized control of the county seat of Pagosa Springs. Having been driven into New Mexico, the exiled county commissioners knew that if they did not hold an administrative meeting in Pagosa Springs within 60 days of being elected, they would forfeit their offices. With the desperation of men who stood to lose everything, the deposed family went to work at getting back into town–even though some 75 armed frontiersmen swore that no such thing was going to happen.

  But the Archuletas had one thing the insurgents did not–money. And anyone who had enough wampum had the Pinkerton Detective Agency's ear. When they appeared in James McParland's office with an envelope stuffed with greenbacks, the Archuletas got the Pinkertons interested in their secluded little county. The detective agency's "battle against anarchism" would now head to Pagosa Springs.

Siringo would be the sole agent on the case. His assignment was to infiltrate the rebels' ranks and help the commissioners get into town for their meeting while accumulating any evidence he could against the insurgents in case the conflict went to court. Going by the assumed name of Chas. Anderson, Siringo rode into Pagosa Springs alone. With a boldness that characterized all of his undercover work, Charlie went straight up to the house of E.M. Taylor, the county clerk and the rebellion's leading man, with the intention of boarding in his home. Spinning a tale about being wanted in Texas for killing three Mexicans, Siringo won Taylor's trust after one conversation on his porch. He was sleeping in the enemy's home on the night of the same day he had arrived in town.

The Archuletas made their first move shortly after Charlie had established himself as a sympathizer with the rebellion. Word got out that the county judge, one J. Archuleta, was riding for Pagosa Springs with an attorney and 60 well-armed Mexicans. After quickly throwing together a like number of cowboys and ranchmen, Taylor rode out to meet the judge, stopping the Mexicans' ride on the swift-flowing San Juan River. Siringo was in the rebels' lines when Taylor and Archuleta met on the bridge that led to town. The mood in the mutineers' ranks was boisterous, sustained by generous quantities of whiskey and the intoxicating notion of rebellion. The Coloradans were clearly spoiling for a fight, waving their rifles and yelling obscenities across the river. Archuleta, however, was in no mood for a scrap; after unsuccessful negotiations with Taylor, he ordered his men away from the bridge.

But they did not go as far back as New Mexico. The judge sent word to the rest of the commissioners that he was at the San Juan, and he was soon met by the leaders of the Archuleta family. The officials camped out in an old house on the bank of the river while their little army slept in an abandoned government barracks about a quarter of a mile away. Perhaps the Archuletas believed that they could begin regular negotiations with the townsfolk and reach some kind of peaceful resolution. If so, they had seriously misjudged the mood in Pagosa Springs.

The men in town were not at all interested in talking to the so-called town patriarchs on the other side of the river. As far as they were concerned, once the family was deposed, it was "out of sight, out of mind." But the presence of Mexicans on the edge of town brought back the fire of rebellion, and it was not long before the insurgents, flush with whiskey and hatred, hatched a plot that would rid their county of the Archuletas for good.

It was decided that two men from the town would cross the river a few miles upstream of the Archuletas' camp at 3 AM and creep up on the old house where the commissioners were sleeping. They would quietly ignite a haystack that was up against the building; when the seven officials ran out of their burning shelter, they would be illuminated by the flames and make easy targets for the firing squad that would be waiting with loaded Winchesters on the other side of the river. Amid whoops of joy at their ingenuity, the leaders of the rebellion put off preparations for a few hours and went to Bowland's Saloon for a premature celebration of their rivals' demise. Charlie was with them the entire time.

At about 11 PM, Siringo sneaked away from the others, tore out of town and forded the river half a mile above town. Running into the barracks where the armed Mexicans were camped, he identified himself as a Pinkerton agent and revealed what the rebels had in store for the Archuletas that night. Instructing the guards to give him enough time to get back into Pagosa Springs before moving the officials from the house, Siringo quickly started back for town. He was unaware that the Mexicans had ignored his last instruction–men were sent to get the officials out of their death trap almost as soon as he had left the barracks.

When the rebel guards at the bridge saw the panicked commissioners leaving the house for the barracks under an armed escort, they hastily sent word to Taylor and his compadres, who were still celebrating the imminent deaths of the very men who were now escaping right under their noses. Everyone sobered up during the subsequent head count, during which it was noticed that the town's newcomer, Chas. Anderson, was the only man who was in on the plan and not present. The celebration ended—but the drinking continued. Within a few hours, the saloon was full of surly frontiersmen swearing loudly through ugly drunks. When Siringo wandered into the bar later that night, he could almost hear the gallows creaking in the ominous silence that greeted him.

Pleading innocence amid the shouts for his life, Siringo probably would have been killed that night if it had not been for the good grace of his new friend Taylor. His only defense was a rather lame argument that it would be impossible for him to ford the river and appear in the bar with dry clothes on. Nevertheless, Taylor stood up for the man that was boarding in his house, ignoring the simple fact that Charlie could easily have taken his clothes off when crossing.

The rebels did not kill Charlie that night, but most of them did not believe Siringo's story. Certain that he was a traitor, they began cooking up a plan that would reveal Charlie as an informer for the Archuletas. It was reckoned that if Siringo was a double agent, then he must have connections with Mrs. Scase, wife of one of the county commissioners. She was the only Archuleta relation left in town after the insurrection, having moved into a derelict shack on the river's edge after the rebels burned down her home. And in fact Siringo had been visiting Mrs. Scase daily, depositing reports on his activities and information he had gathered behind an oil painting she had hung up on a wall. Hoping to catch the detective during one of these visits, the rebels stationed two men behind a woodpile near Mrs. Scase's front door.

When Siringo went by Mrs. Scase's place with his report the following night, the two guards stationed at her shack were certain that his game was up. One of the boys bolted back into Pagosa Springs, interrupting a raucous town dance that was being thrown to celebrate the expulsion of the Archuletas. The young man burst into the dance hall, breathless from his run into town. "We got 'im," the youth panted. "That dirty son of a bitch is a spy! He's at old lady Scase's shack right now!"

Without a single order having been given, every man in the hall rushed past the excited messenger. Armed with shotguns, rifles and six-shooters, the men made a beeline for Mrs. Scase's house. Meanwhile, Siringo had hidden his reports and was about to leave the old lady's home. After taking a few minutes to reassure Mrs. Scase that her husband was well and that efforts were being made to bring back the county's elected government, Siringo ducked out the back of the shed through a loose board in the wall that he used as a secret exit. The mob from Pagosa Springs barged into Mrs. Scase's home just as she finished replacing the loose board.

Five minutes later, Siringo nonchalantly walked into the dance hall and instantly knew that he was in trouble. The hall was filled with women and children who began whispering among themselves when he entered. The only men in the building were a couple of fiddle players—and by the looks on their faces, they were staking the odds that two men with fiddles had against one man with a revolver. One boy slipped away to inform the men at the river that Siringo had reappeared in the dance hall.

Before Siringo had time to figure out a plan, the mob came storming back into town. The detective was quickly surrounded by men who were glowering at him from behind cocked guns. By this time, Charlie figured out what had happened and was coolly weighing his options while he did his best to look bewildered. One of his best friends in town, a cattleman named Gordon, stepped forward. "Gordon," Charlie began, " would you mind telling me what in—"

The leathery old rancher interrupted Siringo with a wave of his hand. He looked tired. "Anderson," he said, calling Siringo by his assumed name, "I want to speak to you."

Gordon led the detective into a side room, sat him down and looked at him for a long time before he spoke.

"Anderson, I want you to tell me the truth. If you do, maybe I can save you. Otherwise you are certainly going to be killed. Now, don't lie to me. I want the truth...are you a detective?"

Remembering his cover as a Texas outlaw, Siringo let out a petulant snort. "Hell, no!"

"Well," Gordon replied, "what were you doing in Mrs. Scase's house tonight?"

"Mrs. who?" Charlie put on the best puzzled face he could muster. "I don't know any Mrs. Scase, nor have I ever been in her house."

Siringo was lucky that Mrs. Scase had hung tough and sworn that she did not know anyone named Anderson when the mob crashed into her home. Gordon, however, kept up the interrogation. "Mrs. Scase is married to a corrupt old county commissioner, and one of our men swears he saw you go to her place tonight."

Charlie jumped to his feet, determined to play out the mess he was in like a John Wesley Hardin or Bill Longley would; his hand went for his Colt .45 and he glowered at Gordon. All thoughts of betrayal vanished from the poor rancher's mind as he found himself facing a Texan gunslinger whose name had just been smeared. "Now you show me the dirty whelp who would tell such a lie on me!" Siringo yelled. "If that — good-for-nothing cares to say such a thing to my face, one of us will have to die."

Letting out a long sigh, Gordon put his hand on Siringo's shoulder. The old rancher was an honest man who had made a habit of saying what he meant, so he was not good at doubting the words of others. And besides, he liked Siringo. "I believe, Anderson, that you are telling the truth. But keep cool, and I'll put you face to face with the man."

The pair walked back into the hall where the anxious mob waited. Gordon called forward the young man who had reported Siringo's appearance at the home of Mrs. Scase earlier that night. The crowd went silent as the informant stepped toward Charlie and Gordon. The old rancher was about to ask the guard about what he had seen when Siringo interrupted, loudly so that everyone in the room could hear. "Are you the two-bit liar who says I was down by the river tonight?"

In the face of Siringo's outright defiance, the youth was suddenly uncertain. He had just begun to stammer some kind of response when Charlie interrupted again. "Because, boy, if you're going to be telling such damnable lies, you better be ready to back 'em up!"

Siringo's hand fell to his holster and he glared menacingly as his thumb cocked the hammer of his Peacemaker. The young man tried to stare down Siringo's mock anger, but he did not have the stomach for it. He tried his best to speak steadily. "Well, the man at Mrs. Scase's shack did look a lot like you," he said, his eyes darting to the shooting iron at the detective's hip. "But it being dark, I might have been mistaken."

Though he would never again be above suspicion in Pagosa Springs, Charlie's gutsy stand at the dance hall reminded everyone in town that if he was not an undercover detective, he was a Texan gunslinger—and in a time when ruthless, remorseless killing machines like Ben Thompson, John Wesley Hardin and King Fisher were giving the state's outlaws a fierce reputation, no one was willing to be the man who questioned Siringo's identity. As a matter of fact, Sheriff Dyke was so impressed with Siringo's courage that he appointed the detective as one of his special deputies for the rest of his time in town.

The conflict with the Archuletas ended soon after Bowland's Saloon ran out of whiskey—the townspeople seemed to quickly lose their enthusiasm for rebellion without liquid inspiration. After a few days, the deposed councillors began negotiations with the rebels; the insurgents were promised a share of the county's political spoils and the Archuletas were reestablished in Pagosa Springs. As for Siringo, he resigned his position as deputy sheriff and appeared before a grand jury in Durango, Colorado, where he provided evidence that indicted 16 of the rebellion's leaders.

Most of Siringo's cases played themselves out in this way. Creating a string of undercover identities that ingratiated him to his fugitive charges, Siringo had a remarkable knack for winning the trust of desperate men. After obtaining confessions for whatever crime he was investigating, the cowboy detective's testimony in court would often put away the same men whom he had spent the last few weeks befriending. It was treacherous work, and Siringo had mixed feelings about what he was doing for the Pinkertons. After all, it was Charlie's plebeian roots that allowed him to do his work so well. Many of the men whom Siringo investigated were men much like himself—poor men doing the best they could in the hard conditions of the West. This kind of man often turned to outlawry only because the laws of the land seemed stacked against them. These desperate souls ranged from striking laborers who gave away their lives for pennies in mineshafts while absentee owners got fat off the profits, to train robbers who saw no harm in stealing from railroad barons who procured so much of their wealth through connections in Washington, D.C. Charlie himself blamed "short-horns"—eastern cattle entrepreneurs—for much of the deterioration of the range cattle industry, and he had no love for the get-rich-quick speculators who made their filthy lucre from working men's labor.

So it was that Charlie Siringo, whose assignments were always threatening to contradict his principles, developed ambiguous ideas about his work. He often justified his duplicity as a necessity in his personal vendetta against the forces of anarchy. Nevertheless, there were cases when he could not whitewash the consequences of his actions with ideological excuses—such as the fall of 1887, when Siringo went on the trail of Bill McCoy in the Wyoming Territory. Charlie befriended Tom Hall and his outlaw cowboys at the Keeline Ranch while chasing down McCoy, and he fit in a little too well with the band of renegades. Weeping in drunken misery at the funeral of a gang member's wife, Siringo put on an emotional narration of Mrs. Howard's wake and revealed how close he came to the people he informed against. And while the Pinkerton cowboy detective was diligent in his duties, he was happy that this particular case never saw the light of day because he thought of Hall as "a prince" with "a heart in him like an ox." Nevertheless, when it became obvious that Siringo had been an undercover detective, the gang could not be expected to return his affection despite his own genuine feelings for them.

But Charlie's principles only go so far in explaining his career as a detective. More than any specific belief, what moved Siringo to do what he did was his lust for adventure, and life as a Pinkerton agent provided that in spades. In the years following the McCoy case, Siringo kept busy infiltrating gangs, uncovering mine salting and investigating miners who were stealing ore from their employers.

His next big case started in the winter of 1891. Tension between labor unions and the Mine Owners' Protective Association was mounting along the Coeur d'Alene River in Idaho. Things got ugly in the spring of 1892 when the mine owners reduced wages and the unions responded by declaring a general strike. Vowing never to hire another union man, the mine owners began shipping in scabs from out of state. Spring turned to summer, and as the strike wore on, the starving miners' resentment toward the mine owners and their scabs increased with every new hole they had to punch into their belts. Finally, in July 1892, the workers took up arms against their former employers. In the fight that followed, the strikers added generous doses of dynamite to the western tradition of bullets and buckshot. They attacked the Frisco and Gem mines, then marched on the mines at Bunker Hill and Sullivan. When the smoke cleared, six men were dead, the Frisco mill on the Coeur d'Alene River had been destroyed and all the scabs in the region were captured. It was only when six companies of the National Guard marched into Coeur d'Alene and began making mass arrests of union workers that order was restored in the region. Near the end of 1892, Siringo's firsthand testimony in Coeur d'Alene City would help to convict 18 union leaders for their roles in the violent affair.

    Siringo was first informed of the rising storm in Idaho when James McParland called the cowboy detective into his office early in the winter of 1891. The Mine Owners' Protective Association was bracing itself for the conflict that would inevitably come when miners' salaries were cut. Turning to the Pinkerton agency for help with the upcoming battle, they requested a man who could operate inside union ranks. By this time, McParland considered Siringo his best undercover agent, so he was disappointed when Charlie turned down the assignment because he sympathized with the labor unions in their fight against big capital. Two months later, after the first Pinkerton agent had been run out of the Coeur d'Alene region by suspicious union men, McParland once again appealed to Siringo to take the assignment. This time he gave Siringo the option of observing the state of affairs in the mountains of northern Idaho for himself. If Charlie still felt the same about the struggle after he had infiltrated the union, he would not have to see the assignment through.

Going by the name of C. Leon Allison, Siringo got work in the mining camp of Gem through one of the mine owners' contacts. Charlie was a union member two weeks after he rode into town, and he did so well at rubbing shoulders that he was elected the Gem Union's recording secretary just two months after that. It was while accompanying George A. Pettibone and other union officials on their house calls to scabs who had the misfortune of living in Gem that Siringo's opinion of the conflict in Idaho began to change. After witnessing the harsh rule of union power–under which scabs were often publicly humiliated, violently beaten and even banished from town to fend for themselves in the frigid Idaho winter–Siringo took a new reckoning of the Coeur d'Alene situation. Branding the union men "rabid anarchists," he wrote back to McParland and told his boss that he would stay on the case. Thus Charlie settled down in Gem for what would be the most dangerous assignment in his career as a Pinkerton detective.

Siringo pulled his first stunt in Gem when the Mine Owners' Protective Association began shipping scabs into the region to work the closed-down mines. The union leaders got word of the precise time that one trainload of working men was scheduled to arrive in the town of Wallace. The central union appointed the county sheriff and his small army of union deputies as a welcoming committee and sent them to deal with the incoming workers appropriately. When Siringo learned of the plan, he hastily telegraphed a warning to the men managing the transportation. The train flew by Wallace without stopping, leaving the throng of armed miners who had assembled at the station to stare in helpless disbelief as Sheriff Cunningham galloped after the disappearing locomotive, pathetically waving his arrest warrant at the caboose. The train stopped at Burk, the next town down the tracks, and the miners were hastily marched to a heavily guarded mine before the posse at Wallace could get to them.

Every arrival of non-unionized workers from that day forward came with a cordon of armed guards—and tension along the Coeur d'Alene mounted with every gang of scab miners that got off the train to work the mines in the surrounding canyons.

    Siringo managed to escape any suspicion during the incident in Wallace, but it was not long before the leaders of the central union determined that there was a spy in their midst. The cowboy detective's trouble started late in June 1892. The *Coeur d'Alene Barbarian*, a newspaper that was run by the Mine Owners' Protective Association, published secret information that was known only among leading members of the Gem Union. The union leaders responded by sending in a detective of their own; a few days later, a hired gun named Dallas—a man Siringo described as "a one-eyed, two-legged Irish hyena"—rode into Gem from Butte City, Montana.

    Dallas had been snooping around town for only a few days before he called the Gem Union together for a special meeting. If Siringo was sweating over what might happen that night, his ugly premonition was confirmed when a man named John Murphy approached him in one of Gem's saloons. In a low voice, Murphy warned Siringo that Dallas had singled him out. Charlie had access to all the union's books; he had been making a conspicuous number of trips to the Wallace post office; and he was one of the most recently appointed union officers. Despite all the evidence, John Murphy himself refused to believe that Siringo was a spy. Fidgeting nervously, Murphy leaned close to Charlie. "For your own sake, Allison, you'd best skip out of town as quick as you can. Word is that all hell is gonna break loose any day now, and they want no doubts about anyone's loyalties when things get hot." Murphy downed his whiskey before continuing. "There's been some ugly talk, Allison. You show up tonight and it could be a shallow grave for you."

That Siringo did not turn tail and run after Murphy was finished suggests several possibilities about what kind of man the cowboy detective was—dedicated, fearless or just plain stupid. Laughing in contempt at the young miner's warning, Siringo responded, "Now why should I fear anything, Murphy? I may not be an innocent man, root and branch, but I'll tell you now that I've done nothing wrong against this union. I'm not going anywhere."

By the time union president Oliver Hughes called that night's meeting to order, Siringo—who was seated next to Hughes in front of the sweaty mass of angry miners—may have found himself wishing that he had taken Murphy's advice. When Dallas stepped up on stage, the entire room went suddenly quiet; there was a sense that something dreadful was about to happen. Dallas gave Siringo an ugly look, cleared his throat and began. "Brothers, you have allowed a spy to enter your ranks, and he now sits within reach of my hand. He will never leave this hall alive. You know your duty when it comes to dealing with traitors to our noble cause for the uplifting of mankind. This spy is doomed!"

The room was flooded with thunderous applause—the half-starved miners were eager to see someone, anyone, strung up for their suffering. Charlie found himself clapping along, so hard in fact that his sweaty palms were getting sore. His concealed Colt .45 was heavy in his shoulder holster. Glaring at the posturing Dallas, Siringo knew exactly who his first target would be if it came to shooting. After a lengthy speech on the merits of bravery, vigilance and the union, Dallas called a 10-minute recess. Turning to Hughes, Dallas gestured to where Siringo was sitting, whereupon the president turned to Charlie and said, "Step off the stage, Allison—we've got to look through your book." Siringo felt a hundred murderous glares as he stepped down into the front of the crowd.

The officials were crowded around his book for a few minutes before they found something that interested them.

While the union officials were talking something over, Dallas walked towards Siringo, smug accusation in his eyes. His hand rested on the handle of his revolver with deliberate nonchalance. When the murmuring crowd started to sound hostile, Charlie finally stepped up to the platform. "What's the matter, gentlemen? You seem to be puzzled."

Dallas stepped between Siringo and the union officials. "There's a leaf cut out of this book," he said triumphantly. "We want an explanation."

Thinking quickly, the cowboy detective must have sighed in something close to relief, because he actually had an answer for the men on stage. "Why, Mr. Hughes himself ordered me to cut that leaf out," Siringo answered.

Charlie quickly reminded the union president about the meeting during which they had decided to sabotage the Poorman and Tiger mines by flooding the lower workings of the mineshafts. When the meeting was over, Hughes had told Charlie to tear those minutes of deliberation out of the record and burn them. If Charlie had mailed the incriminating documents to St. Paul instead of destroying them, well, that was something that the men on stage did not need to know. Hughes recalled the incident and backed up Siringo's story. The fire of vengeance died in Dallas' eyes.

Thus Siringo lived through the meeting. The Pinkerton agent's uncanny nerves had foiled Dallas' plan. No doubt Charlie's rival believed Siringo would try to make an escape after the zealous speech to the miners, but not only did the detective stay put, he also maintained such steady composure under the accusations that he convinced everyone present that he was either innocent, fearless or the best liar in the West. Siringo himself later wrote that he got out of the situation by giving the union officials the same poker face he had perfected while playing cards in cowboy camps on the range.

Siringo was still alive, but he was greeted with dark stares of suspicion wherever he went after the union meeting.

Things took a turn for the worse a few days later when a man Siringo knew only as Black Jack rode into town. Charlie had worked undercover to put this man away for bombings in Nevada. Unfortunately, Black Jack had also recognized Siringo, and when the next union meeting came around, the cowboy detective got another warning visit–this time from Billy Flynn, a miner whom Charlie had befriended. Through drunken tears, Flynn told Siringo that Black Jack had pegged Charlie as a Pinkerton detective and that the meeting later that night would surely be his last. This time Siringo heeded the warning.

Charlie wrote a letter of resignation to President Hughes and gave up his union membership, but he did not give up the fight. Staying on in Gem as the strike escalated into warfare, Charlie did all he could for the Mine Owners' Protective Association. He was seen walking in open defiance down the streets of Gem with a loaded Winchester and revolver at his hip. He sneaked across enemy lines to get doctors for beaten scabs and ran information to John Monihan, the superintendent who was managing the ongoing business in the Gem Mine. It was not until the union forces launched their full-scale attack on the Frisco mill that Siringo thought about leaving.

At 6 AM on a bright July morning in 1892, the signal shot was fired for the assault on the mines surrounding Gem. Bullets rained onto the streets of the mining camp as the men barricaded inside the mines returned fire. Meanwhile, a gang of about 50 armed union miners were roaming through Gem, looking for men they did not like; Siringo was at the top of that list.

Charlie probably owed his survival to the fact that his home was built on piles. He sawed a hole in the floor and was able to hide in the narrow three-foot space between the ground and the floorboards underneath the building. Mrs. Shipley, a woman who ran a shop out of the same building, covered the hole with a chest so that when the union mob broke in, Siringo was nowhere to be seen. Listening to the men interrogate Mrs. Shipley and ransack her shop just above him, Siringo heard firsthand their plans for burning "that — Pinkerton spy" at the stake.

Years later, Siringo would write of the fear that seized him at that instant, boasting that he had been unfamiliar with the sensation until that moment. Charlie had heard that men who were scared were not able to spit when stricken by their terror; lying on his stomach underneath his home as guns roared, the Frisco mine burned and the town swarmed with men who wanted to kill him, Siringo tested the theory. When he could not cough up anything but "cotton, or what looked like cotton," it dawned on Charlie that he had his first case of "scared with a big S."

So he promptly began working at getting out of harm's way. Crawling out from beneath his home, Charlie dragged himself under a plank sidewalk that was connected to his house. With the boots of his enemies visible all around him, Siringo kept moving under the walkway until he reached a saloon at the edge of town that was also raised on piles. Charlie darted out from the backside of the bar, and it was only a matter of seconds before he was in the bush and making a beeline for the Gem Mine, which was still held by the owners' men.

Hours after Siringo reached the mine, his employers gave him orders to surrender to the union men, who had the place surrounded. Knowing that he was as good as dead if the miners from town got their hands on him, Siringo and a scab miner named Frank Stark lighted for the hills. The two men made a narrow escape from Gem and lived in the hills around the town of Wallace until the cavalry arrived two days later.

General Carlin marched into Wallace at the head of six full companies of American infantry. Under an edict of martial law, the soldiers began scouring the countryside for union men. They herded more than 300 men into makeshift bullpens that had been quickly erected for the mass arrests. Of course, Siringo helped round up the fleeing union men, relishing the fact that the same people who had been intent on burning him at the stake just a few days earlier were now begging him for mercy. Before the end of the year, Siringo would appear in court and help convict 18 of the union miners on varying charges. Although the Supreme Court would overturn the convictions in 1893, Siringo would always maintain that he did the right thing in fighting down what he saw as brutal union tactics in the silver mines of the Idaho Rockies.

Siringo's adventures were nowhere near over. He had 15 more years with the Pinkertons, most of them spent on the trail of one set of criminals or another. In 1894, he went undercover as a hobo, tramping through Arizona, California, Colorado, New Mexico and Texas. In 1895, he was assigned to chase down a couple of gold thieves who had stolen more than $10,000 from the Treadwell Mine near Juneau, Alaska. During this manhunt, Charlie was navigating not prairie grasses or mountain passes but the rough northern waters of Alaskan straits and inlets. Siringo became such close friends with Charlie Hubbard, one of the men he had been sent to arrest, that once the trap was sprung and it was evident that Siringo had betrayed the gold thief, Hubbard was beside himself. "How in hell can you ever face the public again after the way you treated me?" Hubbard demanded.

In the summer of 1899, Siringo was assigned to Butch Cassidy, the Sundance Kid and their notorious band of robbers. He would chase different members of the gang for four years, and while Siringo's efforts did not amount to any arrests, he foiled more than one of the outfit's plans to rob Union Pacific trains by informing railroad officials as soon as he got wind of the outlaw's intentions.

By 1907, Siringo was tired of dragging his aging bones all over the West in pursuit of depraved outlaws. But Charlie was one of the Pinkerton agency's best agents and James McParland did not want to let him go. He offered the cowboy

CHARLIE SIRINGO HOLDING THE GUN THAT WOUNDED BILLY THE KID

detective a superintendent position, but Siringo declined, saying that "there was not enough kick in office work."

After retiring to his ranch near Santa Fe, New Mexico, Siringo became a writer in his golden years. It was during this time that Charlie's last and most difficult battle would begin. *A Cowboy Detective*, published in 1912, gave detailed description of Pinkerton cases and outraged his former employers. The old cowboy would spend much of the remainder of his life in legal battles with Pinkerton over what he could and could not print.

As bitter as Siringo had become about the Pinkerton organization, *A Cowboy Detective*'s wistful written recollections of the 22 years he spent in the saddle for the company reveal no real regret for the work that he had done. But for a man with a conscience, life as a Pinkerton agent was much more complicated than roping and branding steers. It was not much of leap from being a proud "cowboy detective" to detested "Pinkerton spy," and as Charlie grew older, he became more and more uncertain that he had been on the right side. By 1915, Siringo was so incensed with the Pinkertons that much of his third book, *Two Evil Isms: Pinkertonism and Anarchism*, consisted of a diatribe against his former employer. Again, the Pinkerton agency took Siringo to court over publication of the book.

In December 1922, Siringo fell ill with pleurisy and had to sell his ranch in New Mexico. He moved to San Diego to live with his daughter, Viola Reid, who nursed him back to health. Finally settling down for good in Hollywood, Charlie spent the last years of his life writing *Riata and Spurs*, another nostalgic recollection of life in a West that no longer existed. He died peacefully on October 8, 1928, at 73 years of age.

9

BILL DOOLIN

The Wild Bunch added howls of sadistic joy to the chaotic symphony of bullets and curses that split the air.

The year was 1889, and much of what had been wild about the West was quickly passing into the realm of storybook legend. The once-open cattle range had been fenced in; the abundant short grass that sustained the cattle empires had been used up; the railroads had expanded farther west; and the riotous cowboy had given way to the disciplined homesteader. As the placid farmer replaced the raucous cowpuncher, the dreadful fury of the Sioux Confederacy was subdued under the guns of white civilization and the majestic freedom of the nomadic Native tribes languished within the borders of federal reservations. Forced to adapt to the changing conditions in the West, the remaining inhabitants of the shrinking frontier soon found themselves cast as virtual caricatures in a fading American drama. Cowboys and Indians were now galloping under European pavilions, engaging in mock battles and stagecoach

BILL DOOLIN AS A YOUNG MAN

hold-ups as Buffalo Bill's Wild West Show exported the once-feared denizens of the disappearing frontier to entertain European audiences.

But if the ways of the old frontier were riding into the proverbial sunset, the bang and bluster were not quite out of the West just yet. Minutes before noon on the bright spring day of April 22, 1889, more than 50,000 homesteaders gathered on the borders of the Unassigned Lands, poised to charge into the first of the "land runs" that opened up the Indian Territory to white settlement. At the stroke of noon, army bugles and carbines split the air, and the chaotic rush for land began. Amid the first-come, first-served bedlam of the rush, which ultimately saw thousands of hopeful settlers flood the region with a desperate hunger for land, the Oklahoma Territory was born.

The nascent Oklahoma Territory brought the United States one of the last hurrahs of frontier lawlessness. Along with the droves of settlers came the inevitable gun-toting predators who thrived on frontier instability. Incited by the sudden influx of homesteaders and their money, violent crime in the region swelled to a dramatic peak in the 1890s and then gradually began to ebb. Among the many wicked personalities that rode this final wave of six-gun violence, the individual whose criminal career marked the high tide of banditry in the newly formed territory was a man by the name of Bill Doolin, captain of the infamous Wild Bunch.

Doolin was a man of humble origins who lived most of his short life as an honest laborer. Despite his calm, deliberate nature when in his 20s, he would become a marauding daredevil in his later years. Indeed, few men who met the young Bill Doolin would have guessed that he would embark upon the longest crime spree of any desperado in Oklahoma and star in more murderous and spectacular headlines than any other robber before him. Celebrated as both a scoundrel and folk hero, Doolin was among the last of the old-time gunfighters.

William M. Doolin was born on a farm in Johnson County, Arkansas, in 1858. Only seven years old when his father passed away, Bill grew to adulthood under the yoke of heavy labor, helping his mother on the family farm for the next 17 years of his life. Tall and lanky, Doolin was 23 years old when he finally succumbed to the grand promises of the western horizon and left home for the same elusive opportunities that lured thousands of other young men to the frontier territories of the United States. It was 1882 when Doolin drifted into Caldwell, Kansas, where he met Texan cattleman Oscar D. Halsell, owner of the HH Ranch in the Indian Territory. Taking an instant liking to the laconic young drifter, Halsell hired Doolin onto his outfit on the Cimarron River and introduced the impressionable Arkansan to the rough society on the ranch. Bill soon distinguished himself as a top hand but didn't stay long. He spent the next several years drifting through Montana, Arizona, California and New Mexico, working on different ranches and wandering on whenever the open road called him.

By all accounts, the young Bill Doolin was a man imbued with a peaceful disposition; not until 1888, when he was 30 years old, did Doolin meet the rough group of renegades that would transform him. While working on the Bar X Bar Ranch in the Indian Territory, Bill took up company with a wild group of ne'er-do-wells who soon lured the rootless man into the brutish ways of the gunslinger. Bob, Grat and Emmett Dalton, Dick "Texas Jack" Broadwell, Charley Pierce and George "Bitter Creek" Newcomb–these men formed the rotten core of the infamous Dalton Gang. It is difficult to say whether the dissolute influence of this first-rate collection of six-gun devils put the demon into, or brought the demon out of, Bill Doolin, but under the corrupt tutelage of these gun-toting ruffians, the calm, deliberate demeanor that had endeared him to so many cattlemen in the West gave way to a reckless spirit that could no longer abide the

monotonous life of a rancher. His heart craved action as explosive as the report of a rifle, and it was not long before Doolin became known as the wildest among the unruly band of desperadoes.

Doolin inaugurated his criminal career near the border town of Coffeyville, Kansas, during the Independence Day celebrations of 1891. The sun was setting on July 4 and, with the help of a few kegs of beer, a raucous cowboy celebration was just starting to hit its stride. As the sounds of the full-fledged hoedown spilled through the woods and into Coffeyville, two constables decided to investigate, just to make sure that no laws were being broken in the dry state of Kansas. In the midst of a sudden silence they entered the clearing, and upon seeing the kegs and beer bottles scattered about, the officers demanded to know who owned the illegal alcohol.

A few moments passed before Doolin stood up with a lazy smile on his face and drawled, "Why, that beer don't belong to anyone. It's free, gentlemen–help yourselves."

The constables were not amused by the cowboy's good-natured quip and let it be known that they would have to confiscate the keg, regardless of who owned it. The prospect of losing the lifeblood of the party just as it was getting under way suddenly changed Doolin's outlook toward the officers. His smile dissolved.

With a group of cowboys behind him, Doolin spoke again. "Don't try to take that beer."

What happened next is uncertain. As the constables began to roll one of the kegs away, drunken hands went for their holsters, and both police officers were badly wounded in the ensuing gunfight. Whether Doolin fired the first shots or not is unknown, but he was identified as the leader of the revelry that night, and the law considered him responsible for the shootings. From that day on, Bill Doolin was on the run. Almost inadvertently falling into roguery, once the outlaw's life was thrust upon him he demonstrated a real gift for the senseless violence that marked the gunfighter's days. Doolin accumulated a criminal record with the same zeal that a soldier might collect medals. Years later, when he was finally apprehended, his sins were stacked high and heavy upon that incident from July 4, 1891, when he first went astray.

By September, Bill Doolin was riding with the Dalton Gang. During the tense moments of the train heists at Lelietta, Red Rock and Adair, Doolin exhibited such brash joy that even the dauntless leader of the gang, Bob Dalton, reckoned Bill too reckless for his, and his gang's, own good. When violence erupted at Lelietta and Adair, Doolin seemed to lose his wits: He stormed up and down the station platform, emptying his Winchester and letting loose a volley of joyful profanities. On account of this bent for maniacal glee, Bob excluded Doolin from the ill-fated raid on Coffeyville.

Along with swaggering George Newcomb and Charley Pierce, Bill Doolin was forced to sit aside from the daring, yet disastrous, two-bank hold-up that the Dalton brothers undertook with only the most disciplined members of their gang. On October 5, 1892, Bob Dalton's boys stepped out of the Condon and First National banks into a hail of bullets. With half the town raining lead down on them, the core members of the Dalton Gang were wiped out in a matter of minutes. Young Emmett Dalton was the only survivor of the fiasco; he went on to serve a life sentence at Lansing penitentiary. Not at all daunted by the bloody demise of his former confederates, Doolin gathered Bitter Creek Newcomb and Charley Pierce to their hideout on the Cimarron River. These three men would form the nucleus of an even more depraved band of rogues, now headed by none other than Bill Doolin himself.

Doolin's Wild Bunch began its mischief less than a week after the bloodshed at Coffeyville. On October 12, the following telegram was sent to John J. Kloehr, the man who had killed Grat Dalton during the failed heist:

> Dear Sir:
> I take the time to tell you and the city of Coffeyville that all of the gang ain't dead yet by a hell of a sight and don't you forget it. I would have given all I ever made to have been there on the 5th. There are three of the gang left and we shall come to see you...we shall have revenge for your killing of Bob and Grat and the rest.... You people had no cause to take arms against the gang. The bankers will not help the men that got killed there and you thought you were playing hell fire when you killed three of us, but your time will soon come when you will go into the grave and pass in your checks.... So take warning.
>
> Yours truly,
> DALTON GANG.

The threat was not taken idly. Within hours the panicked town had armed itself in preparation for the assault. A large group of guards and railway agents, bristling with Winchesters, shotguns and six-shooters, fortified the town's train station. Pleas for assistance were telegraphed to Kansas City. A message wired to the mayor of Coffeyville from Detective Fred Dodge in the Indian Territory added fuel to the fire. One of the detective's men had been informed that a band of 40 heavily armed desperadoes had been spotted riding toward the border town, intent on fiery vengeance.

Having drawn all eyes to the keyed-up town, Doolin's gang pulled off its first heist on the night of October 13, robbing the Missouri Pacific Railroad at Caney—18 miles west of the hornets' nest at Coffeyville. Not 40 men, but 3 raided the train: Doolin and Newcomb were joined by the thickset, ill-tempered, swarthy Oliver Yantis, the first newcomer to Doolin's gang. For reasons unknown, Pierce stayed behind at the hideout on the Cimarron while the others made their foray into Kansas.

The next day, after the news of the robbery at nearby Caney got out, the panic at Coffeyville mounted. Everyone was speculating. What was Doolin planning? Was he riding for Coffeyville, attacking everything in his path? How many men did he have under his command? When was the assault coming?

But the attack never came. While the waiting dragged on into the third week of October and posses swarmed all over southeast Kansas, Doolin's small band headed in the opposite direction. They rode toward Garden City more than 200 miles to the northwest, no doubt laughing all the way at the furor their hoax had caused in Coffeyville. The trio arrived in Garden City on October 21 and promptly set about surveying the new region for places where they could exercise their trade. It did not take them long to find a prospect.

On November 1, during the early afternoon of a cold, blustering day, Doolin, Newcomb and Yantis, masked and heavily armed, rode deliberately down the main street of Spearville, a tiny community 17 miles northeast of Dodge. They stopped in front of the Ford County Bank. Doolin and Newcomb stormed into the building while Yantis kept lookout. Less than three minutes later, the bandits were firing shots in the air as they galloped out of town, a bag containing $1697 slung over Newcomb's saddle. Posses were rapidly formed and gave pursuit, but they couldn't keep up with the thoroughbred horses that the outlaws had picked in anticipation of just such a chase. Riding hard all day and throughout the night, the daring trio reached the Oklahoma border by the next morning. Here Doolin and Bitter Creek split up after arranging to meet at their hideout on the Cimarron, while Yantis rode for his sister's home near Orlando. It was the last time Yantis was seen by his partners. By November 30, 1892, four officers had tracked Yantis' trail to his sister's farm, and after a brief gunfight, Yantis lay mortally wounded. His short criminal career had been brought to an abrupt end.

Back at the hideout on the Cimarron, Doolin was marshaling a new group of desperadoes. By the summer of 1893, four gunfighters–George Waightman, Charles Clifton, Bill Blake and Bill Dalton–had joined Doolin, Newcomb and Pierce, swelling the ranks of the Wild Bunch to seven riders. Bill Dalton, brother of Bob, Grat and Emmett, turned his back on farm, family and respectability after Emmett was given a life sentence for his role in the Coffeyville raid. Upon hearing the verdict, which was proclaimed on March 8, Bill Dalton saddled up and headed south to join Doolin, seeking some kind of reckoning with society for the demise of his brothers. Bill Blake, alias Tulsa Jack, was a rough cowboy and gambler whom Doolin had known during his days as an honest rancher. Charles Clifton, alias Dynamite Dick, was no apprentice outlaw. He had a reputation as a cunning and dangerous criminal, having made a living peddling whiskey and rustling horses and cattle around Pauls Valley and Ardmore, Oklahoma. A hot-tempered and fearsome gunfighter, he earned his nickname from his habit of hollowing out the points of his bullets and filling them with dynamite. Finally, there was George "Red Buck" Waightman, a burly, red-haired Texan. He was a horse thief and reputed killer. Red Buck escaped from a federal prison in December 1890 and had been living on the lam for two and a half years before he joined the Wild Bunch. With this roster of accomplished six-gun bandits, Doolin felt confident enough to resume his criminal activity in the Oklahoma Territory.

After midnight on June 11, 1893, five members of the gang–Doolin, Dalton, Newcomb, Tulsa Jack and Dynamite Dick–stormed aboard the New Mexico Express No. 3 on the Santa Fe's Southern California Line near Cimarron, Kansas.

The heist was much more belligerent in tone than the Dalton Gang's operations had been. Gunshots tore through the night as three of the bandits maintained a steady barrage of gunfire on the passenger cars, cursing and hooting at the terrified travelers. The train messenger received a serious wound when the robbers shot their way into the express car. Making off with what turned out to be a meager haul, the gang members vanished into the night as quickly as they had appeared, riding south toward the Oklahoma Territory.

The law was hot on their trails. The Gray County sheriff hastily threw together a posse, and after following the bandits' tracks for scores of miles, concluded that the gang was going to enter the territory north of Fort Supply. Wiring Sheriff Frank Healy at Beaver and Chief Deputy Madsen at Guthrie, the Kansan sheriff reported the route the gang was taking out of his state. So as Doolin's bandits crossed the Kansas border, they were intercepted by Healy and a ragtag posse of six "nesters" that the sheriff had quickly thrown together. However determined Sheriff Healy was, he must have realized that pitting six farmers against five hardened gunfighters did not make for good odds. After the first round of firing, Healy's horse was shot out from under him, and the terrified farmers were sent into a frantic retreat. Nevertheless, Healy did not give up the fight. As the galloping band tore through the flimsy posse, Healy rolled out from under his horse, leveled his Winchester and opened up on the rapidly moving horsemen. Lead whistled around the gang. Suddenly Doolin felt an agonizing jolt up his left leg as a single bullet entered through his heel and tore through to the ball of his foot, shattering the bone. Seeing Doolin lurch in the saddle, Healy knew one of his bullets had found its mark. It was an ugly wound that would never fully heal, leaving Doolin with a pronounced limp for the rest of his days.

The bandits split up to confuse their pursuers after their scrap with Healy. Doolin rode into the shelter of Wolf

Creek and headed southwest, bleeding heavily into his left boot all along the way. It was then that Bill's fame actually worked to his advantage for a change. An impetuous young Arkansan cowboy by the name of Roy Daugherty recognized the badly wounded Doolin when the outlaw rode into his camp after his first day of flight. The star-struck cowboy dressed Doolin's wound and hid him in his tent when marshals rode through looking for the robbers. As soon as he was able, Daugherty took Doolin to the town of Ingalls, the closest place where he knew a doctor he could trust. Daugherty would never go back to cowpunching. The young man stayed on in Ingalls, enthralled by the romance of the outlaw's life. He adopted the moniker "Arkansas Tom" and threw his guns behind the force of the Wild Bunch. It would not be long before his romantic visions of the gunfighter's life were tested under the heavy realities of lead-laden violence.

Located 35 miles northeast of Guthrie, Ingalls became the regular stomping grounds for Doolin's Wild Bunch for a number of reasons. To begin with, Pierce, Newcomb and Doolin had often hidden out at Bill Dunn's homestead, which was only two and a half miles southeast of Ingalls, when they were riding with the Daltons. Bill Dunn and his brothers remained friendly with Doolin's outlaws and allowed the Wild Bunch to lodge in a board-covered storm cave located on their quarter section. Yet strict expedience was not the sole reason for Doolin's attraction to Ingalls. Indeed, breaking what was perhaps the primary rule of the outlaw's code, Bill Doolin fell in love with a woman by the name of Edith Ellsworth. After courting throughout the fall of 1891 and the winter of 1892, the couple were secretly married just before her 20th birthday in March 1893. Though Edith probably suspected that her fiancé was more than a simple cowboy, Doolin made sure that she had no knowledge of his occupation before they were married. Only after their wedding did Doolin come clean with his young bride.

Legend has it that she took the news with surprising poise, gracefully accepting the difficult position as an outlaw's wife. And, for a short time at least, the couple lived in a blissful, if furtive, nuptial happiness.

Over the summer of 1893, the Wild Bunch was in Ingalls regularly. Riding into town to enjoy the fruits of their suspicious labor, they drank, gambled and reveled in the small community for months. Accounts differ on whether the band terrorized or respected the inhabitants of Ingalls. Described as both "likeable fellows" and menacing bullies, they were probably both, depending on whom they were dealing with at any given moment. While roguishness was now second nature to the outlaws, their mischievous tendencies were probably kept in check by the interests they had in town. Not only was Doolin's wife a resident of the borough, but the gang also depended on the cooperation of the citizens there to keep them at arm's length from the law. Thus if the outlaws did occasionally paint the town red during some of those hot summer nights, they most probably did so with more consideration than usually shown by men of their stripe. Nevertheless, the law did eventually sniff Doolin's boys out. And when the men wearing stars came to arrest the band of outlaws, the town of Ingalls trembled under an eruption of violence that completely surpassed any havoc the Wild Bunch may have caused before.

According to legend, a small-time crook known as Ragged Bill gave away the location of Doolin's gang. On the night of June 17, Ragged Bill was on the run after he had clubbed an elderly man in Stillwater and made off with $40. Bob Andrews, the deputy sheriff of Payne County, caught up with the unscrupulous thief while he was sitting at a poker table in Ransom's Saloon in Ingalls. As Ragged Bill was hauled to his feet, he immediately began pleading with the other card players, begging them not to let Andrews drag him into the Stillwater courthouse. Andrews started when he heard Bill refer to the tall man with the drooping mustache as Doolin; it suddenly dawned on the lawman that he stood at the mercy of the most dangerous gang of outlaws in the Oklahoma Territory. Understanding the futility of any kind of forceful escape, he explained why he was on Ragged Bill's trail.

On hearing of the mugger's crime, Doolin snorted, "Anybody who would knock an old man in the head for $40 couldn't carry water for our bunch."

He advised Andrews to cuff his man and, along with Bitter Creek, accompanied the lawman and his captive out of Ingalls. As they reached the edge of town, Doolin said to the deputy, "Andrews, I'm taking your word you won't double-cross me. If you do, we'll meet again sometime." With that, he and Newcomb turned their steeds around and rode back into Ingalls.

Andrews, true to his word, never said anything about his encounter after he returned to Stillwater. But Ragged Bill, locked behind bars, was sour. Loudly cursing Bill Doolin while in jail, he soon revealed the details of his arrest to marshals in Guthrie. By August 31, 1893, two canvas-covered wagons had rolled out of Guthrie in the direction of Ingalls. Each wagon was driven by a single rider, but underneath the white tops were hidden formidable armories—and 13 U.S. deputies bent on the death or capture of Doolin and his boys. Led by Sheriff John Hixon, the expedition camped in a ravine just southwest of Ingalls that night and drew up battle plans for the imminent invasion of the town.

It was 9 AM on September 1, 1893, when word came in to Hixon's camp that Doolin, Dalton, Red Buck, Bitter Creek, Dynamite Dick and Tulsa Jack had just ridden into Ingalls and were in Ransom's Saloon for some early morning whiskey and poker. Suddenly anxious about the odds he was facing, Hixon dispatched a messenger to Stillwater, requesting reinforcements for the raid. In the meantime, he decided to split up his posse to better cover all avenues of escape in case Doolin's boys should think of departing before the men from Stillwater arrived. Hixon's wagon came into town from the south on Oak Street, and his men quietly took up position in the cover of a grove of trees by Dr. D.R. Pickering's home. The other wagon, driven by Dick Speed, rumbled into town from the west. Six heavily armed deputies led by Marshal Tom Hueston surreptitiously tumbled out from under the canvas at the edge of town and set themselves up behind bushes, buildings and fences along the west side of Ash Street. Speed stopped his empty wagon on Ash, just past the Hostetter Feed Barn and Light's Blacksmith Shop.

From Ransom's Saloon, the band had noticed Hixon's wagon from the south, but paid it little mind because Pickering's grove was a popular camping site for travelers. Their suspicions were aroused, however, when they saw Speed's wagon stop up the street. Bitter Creek stepped out to investigate. He saddled up and walked his horse along Ash Street, his eyes peeled for anything unusual. Deputy Speed had dismounted and walked into the feed barn with his Winchester just before Newcomb started out of Ransom's. The deputy was clearing out the barn's two occupants when he noticed George Newcomb carefully riding toward his wagon. Stepping to the doorway, Speed called over young Dell Simmons, who had just walked out of Light's Blacksmith Shop, and asked him to identify the approaching rider. The puzzled boy looked up at Speed's stressed face before exclaiming, "Why, that's Bitter Creek!" Newcomb saw the youngster point in his direction; in the flash of an eye, he pulled his Winchester to his shoulder.

But Speed was faster; in one motion, he threw Simmons behind him and raised his own rifle, sending a bullet ricocheting off of the magazine of Newcomb's weapon and downward into his right leg. Speed's bullet threw Newcomb's rifle off its target; firing a split second later, Newcomb shot wide. His weapon useless, Bitter Creek wheeled his horse around to make his escape while Speed stepped from the doorway of the feed barn to deliver the deathblow. All hell was about to break in Ingalls.

Luckily for Newcomb, Arkansas Tom had spent the night in town. When the first shots of the Ingalls battle were fired, Tom was still in bed up in the garret of the O.K. Hotel instead of swilling whiskey and playing cards at Ransom's. Bolting to the window, Arkansas Tom saw Bitter Creek flicking his horse's reins in a desperate attempt to escape from the sharpshooting deputy. As the lawman stepped forward onto Ash Street and leveled his rifle, the newest member of Doolin's gang opened fire from the top story of the hotel, hitting Speed in the shoulder. The deputy frantically turned for shelter, but never made it back to the feed barn. Arkansas Tom's second shot threw Speed off of his feet, killing him instantly.

Seconds later, pandemonium erupted. Hixon's men in Pickering's grove unleashed a barrage of bullets on Newcomb as he galloped south, madly spurring his horse out of town. The lawmen then came under assault themselves as Doolin, Dalton, Red Buck, Dynamite Dick and Tulsa Jack opened fire from the saloon, covering Bitter Creek's escape. It was raining lead on the streets of Ingalls. Dell Simmons, the same boy whom deputy Speed had questioned at the onset of the battle, was mortally wounded as he ducked out of Vaughn's Saloon; a man by the name of N.A. Walker was shot through the liver when he foolishly ran out onto the street after the shooting started; and a horse tethered outside Ransom's Saloon quietly fell into the dirt, riddled with bullets as the posse returned the fire that came from the saloon. Death visited three men before Newcomb disappeared into the woods, ending the first bout of gunfire.

The lawmen quickly moved into position around Ransom's. Hueston's boys moved down Ash Street. They hunkered down behind the buildings on the west side of the road and trained their weapons on the saloon. Similarly, Hixon's men fanned out from Pickering's grove and soon covered the front of the saloon and the livery stable where the gang's horses were kept. With his posse in position, Hueston yelled out the state of affairs to the besieged party: They were surrounded, with no chance of escape.

Doolin's reply was defiant: "Go to hell!"

All at once, the marshals laid down a ferocious barrage on the saloon. Bullets tore into the building from all sides. The bandits lay flat amid the deadly shower of lead, shattered glass and splintered wood. Old Man Ransom was hit in the leg, and it was soon evident to all that they would not survive if they stayed in the saloon much longer. In a desperate maneuver, Doolin led the gang out of Ransom's by a side door and made a run for the adjoining livery stable. Neil Murray, the bartender at the saloon, paid dearly for the bold tactic. Kicking down the front door of the building, he raised his Winchester to his shoulder to divert the posse's attention from the retreating bandits, but before he could get a single shot away he was hit twice in the ribs and once in the arm. He fell back into the saloon, gravely wounded. As the marshals shifted their position to cover the stable, Arkansas Tom punched a hole through the garret roof of the O.K. Hotel. Standing on a chair and aiming down into the mayhem, he singled out Tom Hueston and fired twice. Two slugs tore into the lawman's belly and left side. Hueston collapsed, and Arkansas Tom had killed his second lawman that morning.

Having made the dash into the barn, the Wild Bunch quickly went to work. Tulsa Jack, Red Buck and Bill Dalton pumped vicious fire at Hixon and his men from the doorway of the barn while Doolin and Dynamite Dick saddled the horses. Minutes later, Doolin and Dynamite Dick burst out the rear door, galloping for the cover of the wooded area to the southwest. Dalton, Red Buck and Tulsa Jack rode out the front door, making a mad dash for the same ravine, which was only a couple of hundred yards away. The trio was waylaid as soon as it charged out the front: A shot fired by Hixon hit Dalton's horse in the jaw, sending the animal spinning away on its hind legs. Struggling to control his mount, Dalton somehow rode on. He was able to spur his horse another 70 yards or so before Deputy Lafe Shadley shot the creature through the leg, shattering the bone. Dalton jumped clear as his mount went down, breaking into a sprint toward the rest of the gang members, who were stopped against the wrong side of a wire fence, maintaining a steady fire at the approaching lawmen. Suddenly aware that the only wire cutters the gang had were in his saddle bag, Dalton halted, swore through his bile and ran back to his fallen horse, exchanging shots with Shadley, who was leading the posse's advance.

Arkansas Tom's Winchester sounded from the hotel attic again. The bullet hit Shadley in the right hip, and as the stricken deputy lurched for cover, Dalton and Arkansas Tom both sent more slugs tearing into him from opposite directions. The brave lawman fell to the ground, mortally wounded, as Dalton reached his horse, grabbed the wire cutters and ran back to the fence under the bandits' heavy cover fire. The posse had slowed its advance after Shadley was shot, giving Dalton a chance to cut through the fence. Before you could say "jackrabbit," the Wild Bunch was tearing away from Ingalls into open country—but there would be two more casualties before the shooting stopped. While the gang was exchanging parting shots, Dynamite Dick took an ugly hit. A bullet lodged in his neck. An innocent onlooker, Frank Biggs, was wounded when a stray bullet passed through his shoulder.

Arkansas Tom staged a fierce, if brief, resistance to the armed marshals when they surrounded the hotel; he surrendered to the law by early afternoon, heartbroken that the boys had not come back for him. A week later, rumors circulated that the Wild Bunch was planning to raid Guthrie and free their confederate. Like Coffeyville a year earlier, Guthrie armed a guard of 40 men and held its breath for three days, expecting an attack. But no rescue party ever came. On May 21, 1894, Arkansas Tom was sentenced to 50 years in prison for his deadly role in the Ingalls fight.

With five killed and five wounded, the battle at Ingalls seemed to quell the rogues' thirst for banditry...for a short time at least. Fall passed into winter, and neither train nor bank was molested by the devilish guns of the Wild Bunch. But Doolin's hiatus from marauding did not last long enough to convince the marshals of Guthrie that any reformation had taken place in the enemy's ranks. By September, Doolin's gang had nursed its wounds, and the Wild Bunch saddled up and rode out among the throng of new homesteaders making the land run into the Cherokee Outlet. There the outlaw band would launch a crime spree that lasted for a year and a half. It would be Bill Doolin's last hurrah.

The year 1894 started with a bang. During the first week of January, Doolin's bandits struck three times, robbing a Clarkson post office, a salesman just south of Stillwater and a messenger for the Nix & Halsell Company west of Perkins. The hits were small and bloodless, but the news that the infamous Wild Bunch was again on the rampage sent tremors through the Oklahoma Territory.

During the afternoon of January 23, Doolin, Bitter Creek and Tulsa Jack galloped into the town of Pawnee on the Cherokee Strip and robbed the Farmers & Citizens Bank at gunpoint. Joined by four other riders when they bolted out of town, the bandits managed to elude a hastily organized posse at Gray Horse Ford. After the incident, Attorney General Richard Olney gave U.S. Marshal Evett Nix authorization to kill, capture or drive Doolin's boys out of the territory, using whatever public money was necessary. The hunt was on.

Meanwhile, Doolin recruited two more gunslingers to his band: William F. Raidler, alias Little Bill, and Richard West, alias Little Dick. Raidler was a well-educated Pennsylvanian who had become a good friend of Doolin's while working on Oscar Halsell's ranches. West was worlds apart from Raidler. He had been a drifter as long as he could remember. An orphan at a young age, Little Dick was known to say, "I was just dropped on the prairie somewhere." The necessities of survival in that harsh land had hardened West's character, and he had grown into a wild, ill-tempered young man who was full of hostility.

Bill Dalton's last hold-up with the Wild Bunch took place after midnight on Tuesday, March 13, at the railroad depot in Woodward. Bursting into George Rourke's bedroom while he slept, Dalton and Doolin prodded the station agent out of bed with loaded revolvers and marched him to the railroad safe. After emptying the box of its contents, $6450 in cash, the two outlaws quickly mounted up and rode away from the station. They were soon joined by six other riders who had been positioned closely around the rail yard. After the heist that night, Dalton took leave of the Wild Bunch. Either getting nervous at the ever-growing rewards offered for the outlaws' heads or feeling that it was just time to move on, Dalton rode for Texas. He formed his own gang there, but his reign as a bandit king was short-lived; Dalton was hunted down and shot dead on June 8, soon after his band robbed the First National Bank in Longview, Texas.

Meanwhile, Lady Luck continued to ride with the Wild Bunch. At 3 PM on May 10, Doolin, Pierce, Tulsa Jack, Dynamite Dick, Red Buck, Bill Raidler and Dick West thundered into South West City, Missouri, and staged one of the most reckless raids they would ever pull off. The riders reined in their horses in front of the town bank. Three bandits stormed into the building, two stood lookout at the doorway and two guarded the mounts. Within 10 minutes, the three outlaws in the bank came running out with about $3500. Vaulting onto their saddles, they turned to gallop out of town and the air was suddenly alive with gunfire, bullets ricocheting off the buildings around them.

Some of the citizenry had gotten wind of the robbery, and while the outlaws were making their illicit withdrawal, the townsfolk hastily armed themselves for resistance. If Doolin had paused for even a second to assess the situation, the similarity of the unfolding raid to the Daltons' disaster at Coffeyville would likely have elicited a quick prayer from the grizzled man's lips.

But Bill Doolin was not a God-fearing man. The Wild Bunch added howls of sadistic joy to the chaotic symphony of bullets and curses that split the air and, setting spurs to flanks, began a brutal ride through the streets of South West City. Firing on anyone foolhardy enough to try to stop them, the bandits cut a bloody swath through the streets of the small town. Mart Pembree slumped to the ground, a bullet shattering his leg. Deputy U.S. Marshal Simpson Melton fell, shot through the thigh, as he continued to fire on the escaping band. Little Bill Raidler trained his six-shooter on a couple of men who were running out of a hardware store and fired once. His bullet passed through Oscar Seaborn's body and into his brother, J.C. Seaborn. Oscar was badly wounded; J.C. would soon die. Leaving carnage in their wake, the seven riders tore out of town–not one of them having sustained an injury.

Yet Fortune is a fickle mistress, and those who constantly rely on her favor are eventually spurned. Certainly Doolin, a gambler and gunman, knew her capricious nature all too well. After the experience in South West City, he must have decided that he had asked more of Lady Luck than most men do in a lifetime, and for nearly one year, he ordered his band to lie low.

But the rest of the year did not pass uneventfully. Marshal Nix was hell-bent on the capture of Doolin's gang. He put two of the territory's most astute lawmen, Bill Tilghman and Heck Thomas, on Doolin's trail. Hunted by the law throughout 1894, the Wild Bunch had more than one close call but always seemed to emerge unscathed.

The desperadoes did not work alone. Doolin was quite a popular man in much of the Oklahoma Territory. Capable of remarkable generosity, the bandit leader often helped homesteaders through tough times, giving them money for groceries during the early years of their settlement. Thus, despite the large price on his head, locals would warn him of approaching posses and even offer shelter when things got tight.

Given the loyalty Doolin inspired in so many country folk, it is ironic that the homesteading family he trusted most would largely be responsible for the ruin of his band. During the course of the manhunt for the bandits, it became known that Bill Dunn was often in close contact with the Wild Bunch. Dunn had been a friend of Doolin's since 1891, when he was still riding with the Dalton Gang. Tilghman got in touch with Dunn in the winter of 1895 and offered to lift a cattle-rustling charge against him and his brothers if Dunn would cooperate in wiping out Doolin's gang. Dunn agreed, and from that day forward one of Doolin's closest friends was conspiring against him.

The gang's last raid took place on the moonlit evening of April 3, 1895, and was staged without Doolin. Newcomb, Pierce, Tulsa Jack, Red Buck and Little Bill boarded the Rock Island train at Dover, about nine miles north of Kingfisher. The band went about its looting with composure. Except for a little gunplay with the express messenger and some difficulties in cracking the safe, the hold-up went smoothly. After relieving the passengers of their valuables, the rogues disappeared into the night, whooping it up as they galloped away.

The law was soon after them. That same night, the details of the robbery were telegraphed to lawmen in El Reno. The Rock Island Railroad promptly put out a reward of $1000 on each of the bandits. By 3 AM, 12 deputy marshals, with their horses and guns in tow, got off the train at Kingfisher, intent on the death or capture of the band of robbers. Led by Chris Madsen, it was the posse that would break up the Wild Bunch for good. The lawmen picked up the gang's trail early that morning and caught up with Doolin's boys at about 2 PM, practically stumbling on the bandits while they were resting in a small grove of blackjacks. The outlaws scrambled for cover in the trees, and in a matter of moments, weapons were drawn and the two groups were locked in a frenzied gunfight that lasted for the better part of an hour. By the time the outlaws raced away, their delusions of invulnerability had been shattered. Tulsa Jack lay dead, a Winchester ball through his heart. Little Bill Raidler had been dealt a gruesome blow when one of his fingers was pulverized by a rifle bullet.

After a day-long chase, the gang split up in the foothills of the Glass Mountains on April 5, never to reunite. A month later, Bitter Creek Newcomb and Charley Pierce were ambushed by the treacherous Bill and John Dunn while riding into the Dunn ranch. The two turncoats opened up on the bandits when they dismounted in Dunn's yard, shooting the pair of outlaws dead before they could even draw their guns.

Bill Dalton, Tulsa Jack, Bitter Creek Newcomb, Charley Pierce—as the law whittled down the Wild Bunch, Doolin could no longer ignore the writing on the wall. Evidently, the bandit leader's greatest concern was for his family. Edith was still waiting for Bill at her father's home in Lawson, and she was not alone—she was raising the couple's two-year-old son, a boy whom Doolin had scarcely seen while on his larcenous campaigns across Oklahoma and

Kansas. And even if the push of violence and pull of family were not enough to turn Doolin from his wild ways, he now had a painful rheumatism in his left leg, a nagging problem that had developed over the previous year as a result of the bullet he had taken in the foot after the Cimarron robbery in 1893. Suddenly seized by a desire to "lead the right kind of life," Doolin began plotting some kind of escape from the outlawry that had been his stock in trade since that July night in 1891. On a few occasions, he even went so far as to try to make a deal with Marshal Nix, offering to surrender in exchange for a lenient sentence. The determined Nix refused all of Doolin's advances.

So Doolin headed west for New Mexico to join Little Dick West on Eugene Rhodes' ranch. Dubbed "Outlaw's Paradise," Rhodes' outfit housed a great number of renegades who worked for the famed cattleman while hiding from the law. Doolin did not stay long in New Mexico, however. Living in Eugene Rhodes' limbo, a life in hiding where nothing was resolved and anything was possible, did not appeal to Doolin's active personality at all. After he got word of Tilghman capturing Little Bill in Osage country, the wily outlaw decided it was time for him to take his own gamble–either he would make an escape with wife and son, winning back the freedom to choose a decent life, or he would fail in the attempt and suffer the consequences. Setting out on one of his final gambits, Doolin left New Mexico in September 1895, scheming to reunite himself with his family.

But by now, there was too much heat. When Edith and her son vanished from Lawson in the fall of 1895, Tilghman was instantly on the case. Before the year was over, he had tracked Mrs. Doolin to Burden, Kansas, a small community in the Flint Hills. Tilghman's sources were correct; Doolin was living in Burden with his wife during the last months of the year. But just before Tilghman reached town,

Doolin—exhibiting either extraordinary intuition or just plain dumb luck—vanished. Undaunted, Tilghman began snooping through Burden and three days later was again hot on the outlaw's trail.

Tilghman arrested Bill Doolin in Eureka Springs, Arkansas, on January 15, 1896. Doolin, who was visiting the springs for his rheumatism, was reading a paper in the waiting room of a bathhouse when Tilghman got the jump on him. Though the muzzle of a Peacemaker was practically pressed against his forehead, the bandit feigned innocence, declaring that Tilghman was mistaking him for someone else.

The resolute lawman stared straight into Doolin's eyes and responded tersely, "Now, look at me—don't you know me?"

A smile crept across Doolin's face; he knew perfectly well who the lawman in front of him was and even had a grudging respect for the man. He confessed, "Yes, I know you are Tilghman." Looking across the room behind the deputy, he asked, "Where are your other men?"

Thus one of the most infamous outlaws in the West was captured by a solitary peace officer, and not a single shot was fired.

Tilghman brought Doolin into Guthrie the next day. He was greeted by more than 2000 people at the train station, all clamoring to get a look at the legendary bandit king. For his part, Doolin greeted the crowd with surprisingly good humor. The people who came expecting to see a scarred, scowling, tobacco-chewing villain must have been astonished. Wearing a suit, his hands unbound, favoring his right leg and walking with a cane, Doolin ambled into the throng with the practiced poise of a political candidate, shaking hands and exchanging short pleasantries with the town's gentry. Late into the evening, Doolin entertained scores of reporters in his cell, spinning tales of the cow-puncher's rugged life on the range. Regarding the charges against him, Doolin responded, "If I had been in all the raids and battles ascribed to me, it would make a very interesting story. But because I was not in them, I have nothing to tell. I'm glad that I'll now have a chance to prove myself innocent."

By May 1, Red Buck Waightman had been shot to death in a gunfight with deputy marshals near the town of Arapaho, Oklahoma, and Dynamite Dick had been arrested on whiskey charges in Paris, Texas. Doolin, having made a deal with the U.S. district attorney that would get him 50 years in prison, was about to plead guilty to the killings of marshals Speed, Hueston and Shadley during the Ingalls battle. During the arraignment, however, Doolin backed out of the agreement and pleaded not guilty to the charges. After a date for the trial was set, the outlaw was led out of the courtroom under the astonished stares of the authorities. On their way back to prison, Tilghman looked over at his charge. "Bill, why did you go back on your word?" he asked.

Obviously mulling over what he had just done, Doolin responded, "Well, 50 years seems a mighty long time. Besides," he added with a crooked smile, "I think I might know how to beat those charges."

Doolin was not talking about legal loopholes. On the night of July 5, 1896, with the help of the other inmates, the bandit chief orchestrated a prison break. While night guards Joe Miller and J.T. Tull were making their rounds through the bullpen, the inmates rushed them. One hulking prisoner named George Lane reached out for the water bucket as Tull passed his cell. Suddenly lunging, the inmate grabbed Tull's arms and pinned him to the bars. Lane's cellmates quickly disarmed Tull. Meanwhile, Doolin, who on account of a feigned illness had been allowed to spend his days in the bullpen, quickly rushed out through the doorway, locking Miller and Tull in the room with the convicts. Arming himself with Miller's six-shooter, which had been left in a box just outside, Doolin walked back into the bullpen, where the guards now stood helpless. After Doolin had pistol-whipped Bill Dean, a prison trustee who came to Tull's aid, he pressed his cocked six-shooter to Tull's temple and ordered the guard to open the combination locks that held the convicts. Among the eight prisoners that darted out of their cells was Doolin's long-time confederate, Dynamite Dick. Led by Dick and Doolin, the criminals crept out into the night, leaving Guthrie as quickly as they could. The law was after the escapees in a matter of hours, but aside from William Beck, who turned himself in after reaching the outskirts of town, all the convicts vanished. Only two of them were ever recaptured.

While the entire territory was abuzz with the news of Doolin's escape, the law resolutely went back to the dangerous business of hunting the famous gunslinger down. Heck Thomas, deputy U.S. marshal and an expert manhunter, did not waste any time. Before setting out to scout Doolin's old haunts along the Cimarron River, he got in touch with Bill Dunn, ordering him to keep an eye on the movements of Edith Doolin in Lawson.

Sure enough, Doolin reappeared in Edith's hometown. Still clinging to his dream of an honest life with his wife and son, Doolin quietly rode into town on the night of Sunday, August 23, 1896. Stealing into his wife's home and staying until late the next morning, the outlaw went over his plans to leave the country. Soon after his departure, Edith and her father began loading a wagon for a long journey.

Their activities did not go unnoticed. Bill Dunn had offered two young blacksmiths, Tom and Charlie Noble, a cut of the reward if they were able to contribute to Doolin's arrest. The brothers lived across the street from Mrs. Doolin and were diligent in keeping close watch over the house. They promptly sent a messenger to Dunn's ranch, and by

August 25, Heck Thomas' posse had joined the Noble boys and Bill, Dal, George and John Dunn just outside of Lawson. As night fell, the group crept through the town, taking up positions around Mrs. Doolin's home.

Bill and Edith Doolin were making the final preparations for their escape in the stable behind the Ellsworth post office. Doolin must have been suspicious of something, because he told her to ride ahead in the wagon and wait at a spring that was two miles out of town. As Edith dashed through the moonlit streets of Lawson, Doolin began his deliberate march out of town, leading his horse by the reins with one hand, holding a Winchester in the other. His eyes peered carefully into the darkness.

As he drew close to where Heck Thomas was hiding, the lawman hollered, "Halt, Bill!" from the darkness. But before Heck could raise his shotgun, Doolin leveled his Winchester and sent two shots in the direction of the voice. One bullet narrowly missed the lawman, whistling between Bill Dunn and Thomas. Across the street, the other group of lawmen yelled, "Stop, throw up your hands!"

With his dream of escape so close, Doolin was determined not to go back to prison. Whirling around, he fired another round from his rifle. He was just about to jerk his six-shooter when the posse responded. Two shots were fired wide before Heck Thomas' shotgun blast tore through Doolin's chest, killing him instantly. As he collapsed into the dirt, the entire town heard Edith Doolin scream, "Oh, my God, they have killed him!" Leaping from the wagon, she ran back to her husband's still-warm corpse; his chest had been drilled with 21 pieces of buckshot.

The remainder of the Wild Bunch did not last long after Doolin's death. In December of that same year, Dynamite Dick met a violent end. Finally hunted down by a posse that had been on his trail for weeks, the outlaw died with his boots on in a gunfight near Newkirk, Oklahoma.

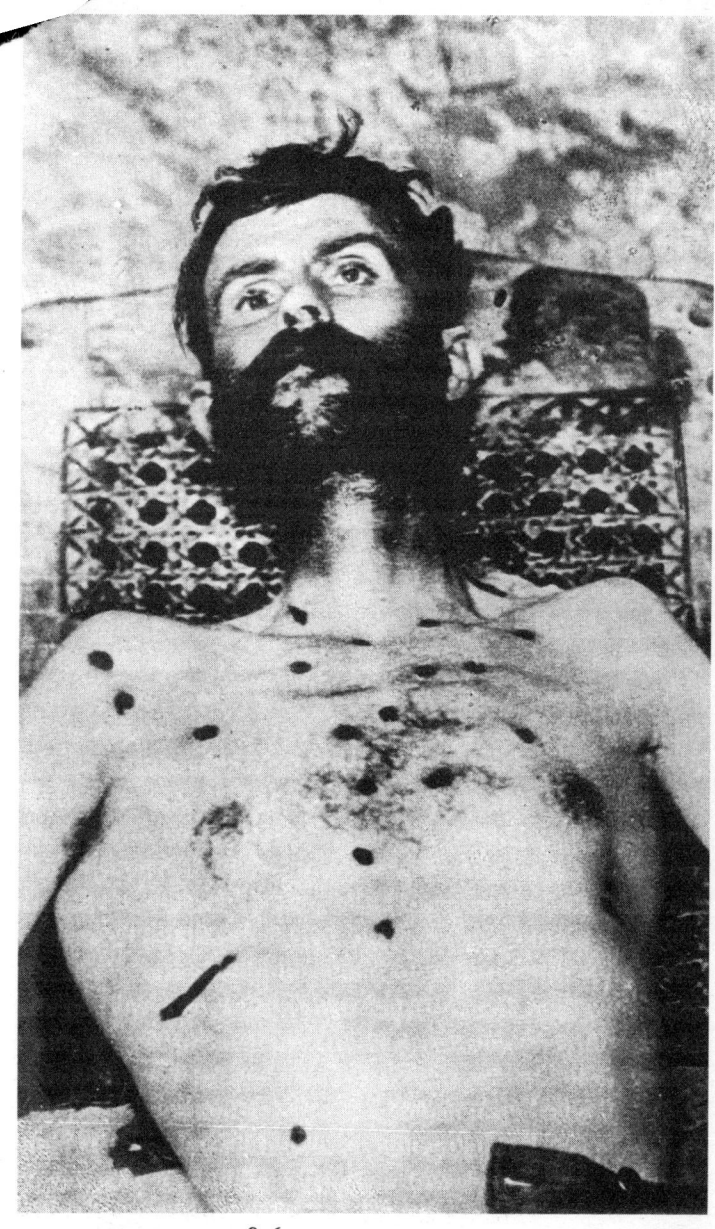

BILL DOOLIN IN DEATH, 1896

Little Dick West, the last active member of the Wild Bunch, took part in a few unsuccessful heists before he was shot to death just outside of Guthrie on April 8, 1898.

While violent crime continued in Oklahoma through the turn of the century, the passing of the Wild Bunch marked the end of an era. The bandana-masked desperado with cowboy hat and six-shooters, riding in hard on a train or bank, was fading into history; nevertheless, that dashing breed of criminal who terrorized law-abiding citizens of the frontier during the last half of the 19th century would not be forgotten. Bill Doolin was soon enshrined as one of the premier figures in that dubious pantheon of western gunslingers, who, mixing honor and greed, fought to live and lived to fight.